# Japan

## by Dorothy Menpes

TO MY FRIEND

THE LADY EDWARD CECIL

TO WHOSE ENTHUSIASTIC SYMPATHY MY WORK IN JAPAN OWES SO MUCH
OF THE SUCCESS IT HAS ATTAINED

Note

In this book I endeavour to present, with whatever skill of penmanship I may possess, my father's impressions of Japan. I trust that they will not lose in force and vigour in that they are closely intermingled with my own impressions, which were none the less vivid because they were those of a child,--for it was as a child, keenly interested in and enjoying all I saw, that I passed, four or five years ago, through that lovely flower-land of the Far East, which my father has here so charmingly memorialised in colour.

DOROTHY MENPES

November 1901.

Contents

CHAPTER I

ART AND THE DRAMA

I always agree with that man who said, "Let me make the nation's songs and I care not who frames her laws," or words to that effect, for, in my opinion, nothing so well indicates national character or so keenly accentuates the difference between individuals and nations as the way in which they spend their leisure hours; and the theatres of Japan are thoroughly typical of the people's character. It would be utterly impossible for the Japanese to keep art out of their lives. It creeps into everything, and is as the very air they breathe. Art with them is not only a conscious effort to achieve the beautiful, but also an instinctive expression of inherited taste. It beautifies their homes and pervades their gardens; and perhaps one never realises this all-dominating power more fully than when in a Japanese theatre, which is, invariably, a veritable temple of art. But here with us in the West it is different. We have no art, and our methods merely lead us to deception, while we do not begin to understand those few great truths which form the basis of oriental philosophy, and without which perfection in the dramatic art is impossible. For example, the philosophy of balance, of which the Japanese are past masters, is to us unknown. The fact that Nature is commonplace, thereby forming a background, as it were, for Tragedy and the spirit of life to work, has never occurred to us; while the background of our Western play is not by any means a plan created by a true artist upon which to display the dramatic picture as it is in Japan, but simply a background to advertise the stage-manager's imitative talent. The result is, of course, that the acting and the environment are at variance instead of being in harmonic unity. But we in the West have not time to think of vague things, such as balance and breadth and the creating of pictures. What we want is realism; we want a sky to look like a real sky, and the moon in it to look like a real moon, even if it travels by clock-work, as it has been known to do occasionally. And so real is this clock-work moon that we are deceived into imagining that it is the moon, the actual moon. But the deception is not pleasant; in fact, it almost gives you indigestion to see a moon, and such a moon, careering over the whole sky in half an hour. In Japan they would not occupy themselves with making you believe that a moon on the stage was a real one--they would consider such false realism as a bit of gross degradation--but they would take the greatest possible pains as to the proper placing of that palpably pasteboard moon of theirs, even if they had to hold it up in the sky by the aid of a broom-stick.

In Japan the scenic work of a play is handled by one man alone, and that man is the dramatic author, who is almost invariably a great artist. To him the stage is a huge canvas upon which he is to paint his picture, and of which each actor forms a component part. This picture of his has to be thought out in every detail; he has to think of his figures in relation to his background, just as a Japanese architect when building a house or a temple takes into consideration the surrounding scenery, and even the trees and the hills, in order to form a complete picture, perfect in balance and in form. When a dramatic author places his drama upon the stage, he arranges the colour and setting of it in obedience to his ideas of fitness, which are partly intuitive and partly traditional. It is probably necessary that his background should be a monotone, or arranged in broad masses of colour, in order to balance the brilliancy of the action, and against which the moving figures are sharply defined. And it is only in Japan that you see such brilliant luminous effects on the stage, for the Japs alone seem to have the courage to handle very vivid colours in a masterly way--glorious sweeps of gold and of blue--vivid, positive colour. No low-toned plush curtains and what we call rich, sombre colour, with overdressed, shifted-calved flunkeys, stepping silently about on velvet carpets, shod in list slippers, and looking for all the world like a lot of burglars, only needing a couple of dark lanterns to complete their stealthy appearance.

Then, there are no Morris-papered anterooms and corridors in Japan, as we have here--sad bottlegreens and browns leading to a stage that is still sadder in colour--only a sadness lit up by a fierce glare of electric light.

The true artistic spirit is wanting in the West. We are too timid to deal in masses for effect, and we have such a craving for realism that we become simply technical imitators like the counterfeiters of banknotes. Our great and all-prevailing idea is to cram as much of what we call realism and detail into a scene as possible; the richer the company, and the more money they have to handle, the more hopeless the work becomes, for the degradation of it is still more forcibly emphasised. Consequently, we always create spotty pictures; in fact, one rarely ever sees a well-balanced scene in a Western theatre, and simply because we do not realise the breadth and simplicity of Nature. There are not the violent contrasts in Nature that our artists are so continually depicting: Nature plays well within her range, and you seldom see her going to extremes. In a sunlit garden the deepest shadow and the brightest light come very near together, so broad and so subtle are her harmonies. We do not realise this, and we sacrifice breadth in the vain endeavour to gain what we propose to call strength--strength is sharp; but breadth is quiet and full of reserve. None understands this simple truth so well as the Japanese. It forms the very basis of oriental philosophy, and through the true perception of it they have attained to those ideas of balance which are so eminent a characteristic of Japanese art.

When you have balanced force you have reached perfection, and this is of course the true criterion of dramatic art. But here in the West we must be realistic, and if a manager succeeds in producing upon the stage an exact representation of a room in Belgrave Square he is perfectly content, and looks upon his work as a triumph. There is to be no choice: he does not choose his room from the decorative standpoint--such a thing would never occur to him for a moment--but simply grabs at this particular room that he happens to know in Belgrave Square, nicknacks and all, and plants it upon the stage. His wife, he imagines, has a taste for dress, and she dresses the people that are to sit about in this room, probably playing a game of "Bridge," just as you might see it played any day in Belgrave Square. I remember once, when a play of this nature was being acted at one of our leading theatres, hearing a disgusted exclamation from a man at my side--"Well! if that's all," he growled, "we might go and see a game of Bridge played any night"; and it occurred to me as I heard him that the managers will suffer for this foolish realism, the public will soon tire of it, for they, almost unconsciously, want something altogether bigger and finer--let us hope they want art.

The Japanese are not led away by this struggle to be realistic, and this is one of the chief reasons why the stage of Japan is so far ahead of our stage. If a horse is introduced into a scene he will be by no means a real horse, but a very wooden one, with wooden joints, just like a nursery rocking-horse; yet this decorative animal will be certain to take its proper place in the composition of the picture. But when realism has its artistic value, the Japs will use it to the full. If a scene is to be the interior of a house, it will be an interior, complete in every detail down to the exquisite bowl of flowers which almost invariably forms the chief decoration of a Japanese room. But suppose they want a garden: they do not proceed, as we do, to take one special garden and copy it literally; that garden has to be created and thought out to form a perfect whole; even the lines of the tiny trees and the shape of the hills in the distance have to be considered in relation to the figures of the actors who are to tell their story there. This is true art. Then, when you go to a theatre in Japan, you are made to feel that you are actually living in the atmosphere of the play: the body of the theatre and the stage are linked together, and the spectator feels that he is contained in the picture itself, that he is looking on at a scene which is taking place in real life just before his very eyes. And it is the great aim of every ambitious dramatic author to make you feel this. To gain this end, if the scene is situated by the seashore, he will cause the sea, which is represented by that decorative design called the wave pattern, to be swept right round the theatre, embracing both audience and stage and dragging you into the very heart of his picture.

For this same reason, a Japanese theatre is always built with two broad passages, called Hanamichi (or flower-paths), leading through the audience to the stage, up which you can watch a Daimio and his gorgeous retinue sweep on his royal way to visit perhaps another Daimio whose house is represented on the stage. This is very dramatic, and greatly forwards the author's scheme of bringing you into touch with the stage. But we in our Western theatres need not trouble ourselves with all this, for we frame our scenes in a vulgar gilt frame; we hem them in and cut them off from the rest of the house. When we go to a theatre here, we go to view a picture hung up on a wall, and generally a very foolish inartistic picture it is too. And even taking our stage from the point of view of a picture, it is wrong, for in a work of art the frame should never have an independent value as an achievement, but be subordinate to, and part of, the whole. All idea of framing the stage must be done away with; else we are in danger of going to the other extreme, as some artists have done, and cause our picture to overlap and spread itself upon the frame. An artist in a realistic mood has been known, when painting a picture of the seaside, to so crave after texture as to sprinkle sand upon the foreground, and becoming more and more enthusiastic he has at last ended in an exuberance of realism by clapping some real shells on to the frame and gilding them over. Thus the picture appeared to pour out on to its frame. This is all very terrible and inartistic; yet it is but an instance of the kind of mistake that we let ourselves in for by the ridiculous method of stage-setting which we practise.

Now, built as the Japanese theatres are, with their flower-paths leading from the stage, there is no fear of such a disaster; yet Westerners, who have never been to Japan, on hearing of the construction of a Japanese theatre, are rather inclined to conjure up to their fancies visions of the low comedian who springs through trap-doors, and of the clown who leaves the ring of the circus to seat himself between two maiden ladies in the audience; but if these people were to go to Japan and see a really fine production at a properly conducted theatre, such an idea would never occur to them at all.

Here and there, however, the unthinking globe-trotter, with more or less the vulgar mind, will be inclined to laugh as he sees a richly-clothed actor sweep majestically through the audience to the stage; he will point out the prompter who never attempts to conceal himself, and the little black-robed supers who career about the stage arranging dresses, slipping stools under actors, and bearing away any little article that they don't happen to want. "How funny and elementary it all is!" they will remark; but there is nothing elementary about it at all; these little supers who appear to them so amusing are perfect little artists, and are absolutely necessary to ensure the success of a scene. Suppose Danjuro, the greatest actor in Japan, appears upon the stage dressed in a most gorgeous costume, and takes up a position before a screen which he will probably have to retain for half an hour: these little people must be there to see that the sweep of his dress is correct in relation to the lines of the screen. The placing of this drapery is elaborately rehearsed by the supers, and when they step back from their work even the globe-trotter is bound to admit that the picture created by Danjuro and the screen is a perfectly beautiful one, and a picture which could not have been brought about by merely walking up and stopping short, or by the backward kick that a leading lady gives to her skirt. These little supers may go, come, and drift about on the stage; they may slip props under the actors and illuminate their faces with torches; yet the refined Japanese gentleman (and he is always an artist) is utterly unconscious of their presence. They are dressed in black: therefore it would be considered as the height of vulgarity in him to see them. Indeed, the audience are in honour bound not to notice these people, and it would be deemed in their eyes just as vulgar for you to point out a super in the act of arranging a bit of drapery, as to enter a temple and smell the incense there. No Japanese ever smells incense: he is merely conscious of it. Incense is full of divine and beautiful suggestion; but the moment you begin to vulgarise it by talking, or even thinking, of its smell, all beauty and significance is destroyed.

Everything connected with the stage in Japan is reduced to a fine art: the actor's walk--the dignity of it!--you would never see a man walk in the street as he would on the stage. And then the tone of voice, bearing, and attitude--everything about the man is changed. I remember once in Tokio being introduced to the manager of a local theatre, whose performance so much pleased me that I begged the privilege of making a few studies before the play began, hinting at the same time that I should very much like one or two of the actors to pose for me. Then this little gentleman began to think and frown and pucker his brow, secretly proud that an artist should want to paint his work, and also not unwilling to make a little money. At last, after much deliberation, he decided that I was to have the run of his theatre and ten actors for the afternoon, charging three dollars and a half for the whole concern. This seemed to me to be fairly reasonable; I did not know of any London theatre that I could have hired for three dollars and a half, or even as many pounds, and then the company consisted of ten actors who were all artists, all loving their work as only true artists can. To be sure, it was a suburban theatre, and the acting was not of the finest; probably also there was a great deal of exaggeration in the poses; but still it lent itself to decorative work, and answered my purpose to perfection. They did not act, but merely posed to form a series of pictures, and some of the expressions of the actors were extraordinarily grotesque, just like a Japanese picture-book. But what struck me most of all was the absolute autocracy of the little manager, or whatever he called himself--the Czar of Russia or General Booth was not in it with him for power! He threw his actors about on the stage just as an artist would fling pigment on to a canvas; and his violent whisking of a bit of vermilion and apple-green in against a wave was too dexterous and masterly for anything, and called forth my unfeigned admiration.

The greatest living actor at the present moment in Japan is Danjuro--in fact, I should say that he is one of the greatest actors in the whole world; and in order to give a true insight into the many beauties of the Japanese drama, it seems to me that I cannot do better than describe a day that I once spent with this great master.

I was taken to see him by Fukuchi, Japan's most eminent dramatist and the greatest of living writers. We were shown into a small room with spotless mats to await Danjuro's arrival, and my attention was at once attracted towards an exquisite kakemono that hung on the wall, which was the only decoration the room possessed. It was a picture, a masterpiece, that seemed to suggest one of the early Italian masters; it impressed me tremendously, and I told Fukuchi so. "Ah, I am glad!" he exclaimed, "for Danjuro, the great master, when I told him you were coming and that you were a painter, asked me many questions about you. He took much pains to discover the quality of art that appealed to you, and the side of Nature that you liked the best. He also wished to know your favourite flower, and which kind of blossom you loved the most--whether you preferred, as he did, the single cherry-blossom, or the double. This Danjuro was unable to find out; if he had known he would have chosen a kakemono of flowers for you. But I am glad you like the picture." I was amazed at the kindness of this man Danjuro. There was no accident about this picture that I admired so vastly: it had been chosen for a definite reason--to give me pleasure. And I afterwards learnt that there is no end to the amount of trouble a Japanese gentleman will take in the choosing of the picture that is to hang in the room where you are being entertained.

When you enter a house in Japan, the first and one idea is to give you pleasure, and the people of the house will take elaborate pains, almost the care that a detective will take in detecting a crime, to find out, as delicately as possible, your taste in regard to this picture. They will send their servant round to your hotel to find out what flower you have expressly asked to have placed on your table, and that will be the flower that you will find adorning either a kakemono or a vase when entering the house of your friend.

This room where Fukuchi and I were waiting looked out upon the garden--a miniature garden, no bigger than an ordinary dining-room, yet perfectly balanced, one that held infinite joys: there were the miniature bridges, lakes, and gold-fish, the mountains, the valleys, and the ancient turtles--all correct as to colour and marked by that exquisite taste which only a Japanese landscape-gardener can display. It was a bright sunlit day, and looking from this room with its perfect masterpiece to the little jewel of a garden, you felt that you were living in another world. And it was all so pure and so "right" that I began to feel hopelessly "wrong." It seemed that I was the only blot in these perfect surroundings. And at last I became so shy that I really didn't know what to do with myself, and I felt that the only thing left for me was to take off my clothes and dig a hole in the ground, and then be ashamed that I had left my clothes behind me. However, I controlled my emotions and waited on with Fukuchi until the sliding doors dividing us from the adjoining room were quietly opened and Danjuro appeared. So unlike an actor!--no moving of the eyebrows, no stroking of the hair, but just a simple dignified gentleman, and an old gentleman, quite old. He was a slim, spare man, very refined, with the look of a picture of Buddha by Botticelli. The face was thin and narrow and keen; bright eyes glanced at me from under heavy eyebrows; his manner was magnetic; and I felt at once that he was a great artist. The way his servants saluted him! You could see that they loved him, and yet by the reverence they showed him he might have been a cardinal. I was at once offered exquisite delicacies in little lacquer cups, and we all sat down, on the floor of course, and Danjuro began to talk. One of the first things he said to me, through Fukuchi, who spoke English perfectly, was, "I am told that I have many qualities like your great actor Sir Henry Irving," and even as he spoke I could trace a distinct facial likeness between the two men. His voice was rich and powerful and his enunciation deliberate; he used his hands quietly, and the expression varied very little except when he was anxious to emphasise, and then the change was extraordinary, while the expression and poses were so admirable that I could almost understand what the man was saying.

I instinctively felt that the right thing to do was to first talk of the kakemono, and Danjuro, seeing my genuine enthusiasm, smiled and said, without a touch of false modesty, "Yes; it is a great masterpiece!" and then he began to tell me about this picture, and I felt at once that this dignified little gentleman was a true artist.

From the picture we drifted to the Drama, and Danjuro was very curious to know something of our work in London, and now and then, as he plied me with pertinent questions, I thought I detected a glimmer of fun behind his inscrutable demeanour. At last the questions rained around me so rapidly, and were so terribly to the point, that I felt thoroughly ashamed and did not know how to answer him. I knew that he was an artist, looking at his work from purely the artistic standpoint, and as an artist I knew that it would be utterly impossible for him to appreciate our Western methods: so I deftly turned the conversation by returning the fire of questions. I had seen Danjuro in one or two scenes in which I was greatly struck with the remarkable changes of his facial expression. There was one scene in which Danjuro faced the audience, and in a minute, by the complete alteration of his face, changed himself into an entirely different man. This feat was really so remarkable that I was anxious to know how it was done, and suggested that it might have been accomplished by a clever make-up. "No, no!" he exclaimed. "It is a rule of mine to use 'make-up' very rarely. For change of expression we actors have to depend much on the muscles of our faces"; and Danjuro, to illustrate this, quickly changed his face until it was totally different, even to the face markings, and I should have defied Sherlock Holmes himself to have known him to be the same man. Then I saw him act the part of a drunken man. I have seen drunken men on the stage over and over again, and there has always been a touch of vulgarity about them; but this drunken man of Danjuro's was an exquisite triumph of art. I was curious to know how he had perfected this role and suggested that it had perhaps been brought about through a careful study of the habits and actions of a drunkard, using him as a model, as it were. But this Danjuro firmly denied. "No, no, never!" he exclaimed. "I might just as well take a drunken man and stick him on the stage, just as he is, as to imitate any one man. That is not art: it is not a creation. I have seen drunken men all my life, and the drunken man I represented was the aggregate of all the drunkenness I have ever seen. Suppose by chance I had come across a drunken man while I was developing the character, I should perhaps have been tempted to follow that particular man too closely, and the result would have been necessarily inartistic." And Danjuro made it quite clear to me that when creating the character of either a drunken man or a madman, he invariably keeps as far away from Nature as possible. He would not proceed as some of our actors do, to hunt about In the slums until he had found a man sufficiently drunk for his purpose, and then copy him exactly; or, yet again, he would not have attempted to imitate a death-bed scene by watching one particular person die. Such a thing would appear to him as a great degradation.

Almost imperceptibly the conversation swerved round again to English acting, and Danjuro gave me a rather humorous, though humiliating, description of a play he had seen in Yokohama. The language was gibberish to him, and all he could do was to study the poses of the players, which struck him as being extremely awkward. "They suggested to me badly modelled statues," he explained; "they never seemed to move gracefully, and their actions were always violent and exaggerated." This, from a Japanese, was frank criticism, for he made it quite clear to me that he had little or no sympathy with our methods. He felt that he was talking to an artist and that he could afford to be natural; but after this very candid opinion there was a slight pause, which I hastened to break by putting a question on the subject of his own drama.

The drama of Japan, he told me, was greatly improving; the actors nowadays have chances which in the early days they had not, and it is easier for them to create fine scenic effects. They have the chance of studying great masterpieces at museums; they may copy costumes there, and, above all, they have the superb opportunity of studying colour and form. Then, many of the great Japanese actors possess collections of very fine pictures, while the actors of early times could only study from badly printed woodblocks which were nearly all inaccurate. Schools for actors have been occupying his attention, and he hopes that some day they will be established all over Japan. Actors, in his opinion, should be taught when they are quite young the science of deportment and of graceful movement, to be artists as well as actors, and above all to avoid exaggeration.

Danjuro prefers as an audience the middle classes. "They are more sympathetic," he said; "the diplomats and politicians who have come in touch with the West, and are dressed in European dress, seem somehow to lose sympathy with us, and are not helpful as an audience. Perhaps it is that they can never entirely divest themselves of the sense of their own importance."

After considering Danjuro's views concerning the Japanese drama, I was interested to hear the views of the dramatic author, and Fukuchi and I spent many delightful afternoons together discussing this all-absorbing topic. "What do you claim to be the chief advantages of Japanese as compared with European theatres?" I asked him on one occasion. "Well," replied Fukuchi without a moment's hesitation, "before everything else I should place the Hanamichi (flower-paths). This is absolutely indispensable to the Japanese stage, and allows of endless possibilities. With it we have far greater scope for fine work, and dramatically it is of tremendous advantage. Then there is the revolving stage, which is a great improvement on Western mechanism, for while one scene is being acted, another can be prepared."

On this particular afternoon the dramatist and I were sitting in Mr. Fukuchi's own room overlooking the river with a distant view of the sea. Books, all Japanese, were heaped up in an alcove, while the only furniture the room possessed was a very fine kakemono and a little narrow table. While we were talking, one of Fukuchi's little children, a boy of eight, entered, carrying with him his collection of butterflies, which, he thought, might chance to interest me. He showed me a catalogue which he was preparing for them. It was so admirably compiled that it would have been good enough for a special work on the subject.

Fukuchi's ideal actor is Danjuro, and during the conversation he was constantly referring to him. "Of all the actors I like Danjuro the best," he said, "because he is an artist and understands colour, besides having a keen appreciation for harmony in the general arrangements." He told me that Danjuro is the one actor in Japan who can take the part of a woman to perfection. Many actors on the stage can keep the figure of a woman for five minutes at a time, but rarely longer, so painful are the poses, owing to the throwing back of the shoulders and the turning in of the knees. But Danjuro can go on and on indefinitely in this role and so remarkable is he that even a Japanese woman is unable to detect one false move. On one occasion, when taking this part at a theatre in Yokohama before an audience composed chiefly of women, he happened to make a slip and by some slight error proved himself the man. In an instant the whole audience felt it, and the effect produced on them was simply astounding! For once they nearly laughed, an unheard-of thing with a Japanese audience: to see a woman turn so suddenly into a man was too much for their equanimity.

Danjuro's finest and most artistic bit of acting is in Japan's greatest tragedy, The Chushingura, in the part of Goto, who, returning to his lord intoxicated, falls asleep by the wayside. His master, finding him, fires off a gun close to his ear. "Most actors," said Mr. Fukuchi, "would fall asleep with their backs to the audience, and when waking depend upon 'make-up' for an altered expression. Danjuro sleeps with his face to the audience, and on the gun firing wakes up with an entirely altered expression through the contraction of the facial muscles."

I was curious to know from Fukuchi what were the duties of the stage-manager in Japan. For some time he looked thoughtful, as though unable to grasp my meaning. "We have no managers in Japan," he said at length: "the play has to do with the dramatic author: it is for him to arrange everything. He must first think out every detail, and then consult with the chief actor and proprietor. If these disagree, the play is not produced." Mr. Fukuchi maintained that the dramatic author must be absolute master of the situation, interfered with by none. It would be impossible for an actor or manager to have any conception of the picture as a whole; therefore the dramatist must be supreme. If an actor or an actress were permitted a choice as to the colour or form of costumes, the work would of necessity be ruined. There is no such thing as the leading lady insisting upon wearing a puce dress, as she does in England or anywhere on the Continent. The manager does not know what "puce" means, nor, probably, does the lady; but he sees no reason why she should not wear puce if it pleases her. Accordingly puce is worn, irrespective of scene harmony, and the lady is content. In Japan such an occurrence would be out of the question; but our Western stage is already such a jumble that any little eccentricity on the part of the leading lady in favour of puce or anything else she fancies would be scarcely noticeable.

"They tell me," put in Mr. Fukuchi, "that there are dramatic authors in England who are not artists--that they do not all understand colour harmonies and line. Can this be true?" I had to tell him that such men were not uncommon with us. Fukuchi looked serious, and was silent for a long while, meditating as to how it would be possible for a dramatic author to produce a play without a scientific knowledge of art and drawing. "I fail to understand this," he said after some minutes' thought; "I cannot understand. When I have finished writing my play, and when I have talked with the chief actor, I make my drawings myself. I must make the pictures, and I must give careful directions to the costumiers and the carpenters. I cannot understand how your dramatic author does this." And the little man was genuinely perturbed.

The pictorial side of a Japanese dramatist's work interested me keenly, and I begged Fukuchi to tell me how he, as an author, prepared his drawings for the costumier, stage-painter, and carpenter. "Well, if you like I will show you," he said; "I am now writing a historical play, the scenes of which will be like this," and to my great amazement Fukuchi at once began to draw in a rapid masterly manner the scene of a gentleman's house and garden. No detail, however trivial, was overlooked, and the infinite pains and care with which he executed these delightful little drawings both astonished and charmed me. I could see at once the utter impossibility of any one attempting to interfere with this man, who had a complete grasp of his subject not only from the literary standpoint, but also from the pictorial.

To give any idea of the exquisite delicacy and precision with which these sketches of Fukuchi's were carried out, I must describe one or two of the scenes. First of all there was the garden; this was to have on its right a bamboo fence, a pine-tree, and a grass plot. On the left was placed a willow-tree, and stepping-stones leading from the house to the gate. Then the gentleman's house was to be considered. Mr. Fukuchi decided that this was to be thatched and have a projecting floor, while in front he placed a bamboo fence, a well, and a cluster of chrysanthemums. "Now at the back of the house I must have a range of mountains with autumnal tints," said Fukuchi; and no sooner said than done--in a few minutes there stood the range of mountains with their autumnal tints, ranging from orange to brown, noted in the margin, with directions as to the quality of cotton cloth to be used for their construction. Every detail in this garden scene was exact, and no one could have altered so much as a leaf without ruining the picture. Next Fukuchi proceeded to make for the costumier a drawing of a girl. By the dressing of her hair the girl was shown to be not over nineteen years of age, the ornaments being one of red and the other silver. She was to hold a fan, and Fukuchi even decided on the colour of the fan and the way the girl should hold it. It was to have a gold ground with a silvery moon, light and black grass growing in white water. The lady's kimono was of dark purple at the bottom and light purple at the top; this was arranged purely for decorative reasons in order to harmonise with the obi, which was black. As a rule the colours in a dress graduate from the top downwards; but the obi looked best against the light purple, and custom was sacrificed to art. The figures on the kimono were to be all white with silver strings, and a delicate white wave pattern.

Mr. Fukuchi next proceeded to consider the handling of historical colour. The scene was that of a lord and his wife, the lord just setting out for the wars and the wife seeking to detain him, holding on to his armour. The armour is red and the clothes are indigo. These colours being fixed historically, it was for the artist to arrange backgrounds that should harmonise with these. In the lady alone were his artistic tastes allowed to expand. He would have her dressed in white, with large chrysanthemums in red, yellow, and purple tones.

These exquisitely clothed figures were to be placed before a screen, having sea-rocks and an eagle painted on it with black ink. Yet again another screen was to be of light brown, with glittering birds delicately traced upon it, in order that they should not interfere with the breadth of the whole.

"Now, Mr. Fukuchi," I said, "I can quite see that you are an artist, and that your handling of a play from the decorative standpoint is quite perfect. But now tell me something of your literary methods."

Then Fukuchi began by telling me that in writing a novel he wrote it as a poem, and when writing a play he thought of it as a picture. But there are periods in writing a novel when it in a way gets the better of him, and develops unconsciously into a drama. Then he told me of one or two stories he had recently published, one of which began as a novel and ended as a play. He said he could not understand the habits of some authors of taking down scraps of conversation, and using them for their finished works. He himself spends his whole life listening to conversations and studying the poses of people; but to take notes of what they were saying would be hopeless; the notes could never be used for fine artistic work. In planning a play he sees it as a whole, as a series of pictures, before beginning to pen a line.

I was talking to Fukuchi about realism on the stage, and he told me of the horror they have in Japan of bringing live animals into a play; such a thing has been attempted on one or two occasions, but always with disastrous results. One enterprising actor, he told me, spent much time in training a horse to take part in a very fine production at one of the principal theatres. The horse was trained to perfection, and on the first night that it appeared, being a novelty, it was loudly applauded; but the lights and the confusion so terrified the poor animal that it sat down on the stage and refused to move. Yet again another actor, determined to outdo this former performance in originality, trained a live monkey to take the place of the decorative pasteboard monkey which had always been used on the stage. This animal, unlike the horse, was trained to know the stage as well as his master's room, and grew quite accustomed to the lights and the people surrounding him. So thoroughly at home was this monkey that on its first appearance it swept the stage of all the actors, caused confusion and distress among the audience--in short, it behaved abominably, and did everything but that which it had been so carefully trained to do. After this the pasteboard monkey reigned supreme.

Mr. Fukuchi, although he is a brilliant English scholar and has an intense admiration for Shakspeare's works, thoroughly realises how impossible it would be to attempt to put Hamlet on the Japanese stage: it would suit neither the actors nor the public.

THE LIVING ART

CHAPTER II

THE LIVING ART

A Japanese authority has boasted that the only living art of to-day is the art of Japan; and the remark is not so much exaggerated as it may appear at first sight to the European. Art in Japan is living as art in Greece was living. It forms part and parcel of the very life of the people; every Jap is an artist at heart in the sense that he loves and can understand the beautiful. If one of us could be as fortunate as the man in the story, who came in his voyages upon an island where an Hellenic race preserved all the traditions and all the genius of their Attic ancestors, he would understand what living art really signifies. What would be true of that imaginary Greek island is absolutely true of Japan to-day. Art is in Europe cultivated in the houses of the few, and those few scarcely know either the beauties or the value of the plant they are cultivating. That is the privilege of a class rather than the rightful inheritance of the many. The world is too much divided into the artist on the one hand and the Philistine on the other. But it is not so in Japan, as it was not so in ancient Greece. In Japan the feeling for art is an essential condition of life. This is why I expect so much from the interest in Japan which is now awakening in England.

The report of the Japanese Commission sent to Europe to investigate the conditions of Western art, some years ago, startled Western minds considerably. The Commissioners gave it as their opinion that Japanese art was the only real living art. This surprised, perplexed, and irritated many people, as home truths generally do. Without adopting in integrity every word of the Commission's report, I must confess that I found in it a great deal of truth.

The great characteristic of Japanese art is its intense and extraordinary vitality, in the sense that it is no mere exotic cultivation of the skilful, no mere graceful luxury of the rich, but a part of the daily lives of the people themselves. It is all very well to draw gloomy deductions about the decay of Japanese art from the manufacture and the importation of curios destined for the European market. That there is such an importation there can be no doubt, any more than that this condition of things will continue while people fancy that they are giving proof of their artistic taste by sticking up all over their walls anything and everything, good, bad, and indifferent, which professes to come from Japan or to be made on Japanese models.

What an educated Jap would think of some of our so-called "Japanese rooms" I shudder to imagine. But let me ask--and this is much more to the purpose--what would an uneducated Jap think? And let me give my own answer. He would be as much surprised by any bad taste or bad art as his educated superior would be. This is the burden of my argument--that art in Japan is universal and instructive, and therefore living; not an artificial production of a special class, and therefore not living. Art was certainly a living thing in the best days of Athens; art has been, in some measure, a living thing elsewhere and in later days. For we must remember that art does not merely consist in the production of a certain number of works of art, or even of masterpieces. A country may produce a great many works of art, and yet as a country be entirely lacking in living artistic feeling. France is a land of works of art; but the works do not appeal to the voyou--still less do they appeal to the ouvrier, to the bourgeois, to the butcher, the baker, the candlestick-maker. Now, what I claim for Japan is that in its most real and most important sense it is a living artistic country. The artistic sense is shared by the peasant and the prince, as well as by the carpenter, the fan-maker, the lacquer-worker, and the stateliest daimio whose line dates back to the creation of things.

But do not run away with my contention. I do not mean to say that every Jap is a born artist. There are Philistines in Japan, as elsewhere. What I do maintain is that the artistic instinct is more widely diffused, is more common to all classes of the community in Japan, than in any of our European countries. This is no small thing to say of a country. It is full of deep significance to all students of art. Although we are doing our best, with our love for gimcrackeries, to cheapen and degrade the artistic capacity of Japan, our evil influence has been but partially felt, and so but partially successful. Having done all the harm we can do unwittingly, let us pause, if possible, and reflect before we wittingly do further mischief.

The problem to the lovers of art is simply this: shall we learn all we can learn--and that is a great deal--from the living art instincts of Japan, or shall we continue to blunt and deaden the productive power of Japan by encouraging the barbarous demand for worthless baubles to make ludicrous the home of the so-called aesthete? If those who are most proud of the Japanese toys and trinkets they have amassed, which, with semi-savage stupidity, they have nailed upon their walls and stuck upon their shelves and tables, could but see what an artistic house in Japan is like, they would learn some startling truths as to the real facts and principles of Japanese decoration and the Japanese ideal of art. If they could only know the contempt with which the truly artistic Jap looks upon the demand for "curios," and upon the kind of "curios" which are turned out wholesale to meet that demand, they would not feel so proud of themselves, and of the rooms which they display to delighted friends as "quite Japanese, you know." The artistic Jap shows nothing in a room--absolutely nothing, except a lovely flower and a screen, and perhaps a beautiful verse or some clever sentence indited in freehand writing, placed beautifully in the room in just relation to its surroundings.

There is a curious fact to be noticed in connection with such inscriptions. In conversation a friend might happen to give forth some brilliant and very epigrammatic utterance. The hearers are so delighted that they get him to write down this mot in large characters, and it is mounted and placed in the room. Such a caligraphic maxim, written by the hand of the speaker, they consider a fitting portion of the permanent decoration of a room.

You would never know from the rooms of a Jap that he was a great picture-collector. The wealthy collector keeps all his treasures stowed away in what is called a "go-down"--his storehouse--and his pictures are brought up one at a time if any visitor is present or expected. Generally a single picture will be brought in and hung up. You enjoy that beautiful picture by itself. It is very much like bringing a bottle of wine from the cellar--no one would want the whole bin at a time.

The Japs have an artistic temperament altogether and the simplest craftsman is an artist in his own way. I was especially struck with this once when I was in want of some frames, and I employed a Jap to make them for me. He could talk English perfectly well, and it was remarkable to watch the development of the frames and the enthusiastic temperament discovered by the carpenter as he proceeded. I myself designed a certain frame, and I would by slight drawings encourage him and his fellows to go on with the work. They all took the greatest possible interest in the refinement of the object-- they would place it down and then go off and look at it, and talk to those friends who were looking on about the beauties they saw in it and in its proportions; and the intelligence and pleasure they showed were not only extraordinary but also delightful. This frame-making was quite novel to them, as they do not frame any of their objects; but they were interested in the design of the frame and the placing of the picture within it. Although the matter was not in itself of any remarkable importance, I hold that it fairly proves the artistic temperament of a chance selection of people. Think of a common carpenter making a simple thing and taking a just pride in doing it! The result was that I got one of the most beautiful frames you can conceive, and that I was encouraged in my own work by the sympathy of these workmen.

Of course, in Japan there are painters who paint for the market--people who have been destroyed by the British merchant and the American trader. They spend their time in painting pictures of flowers and birds in vivid colourings that appeal to our tastes, solely for exportation to England and America. Apropos of this I must mention a conversation I had with a painter about screens, which struck me as being very curious. I wanted to buy a gold screen, and he took me to a shop where I saw a vast number of screens, nearly all with black grounds and golden birds and fish on them. I told him I did not like them; and he answered, "Neither do we. Here in Japan we would not have them in our houses; but they are what the English and American markets demand. We ourselves never buy them; we nearly always choose screens with light grounds, beautifully painted"--in fact, splendid pieces of decoration. A screen painted by a first-class artist is valued very highly, while the fact of one from the hand of an old Japanese master being for disposal is known all over the country at once, and everybody is prepared to bid for it as one would bid for a Sir Joshua here. A really good screen fetches an enormous price, for it takes the place there of pictures and frescoes with us, and every man of taste requires one or two fine specimens in his house beautiful. One I saw at the house of the Minister for Foreign Affairs was painted with a blue wave--an arrangement, in fact, in blue and gold. I never saw such a gorgeous screen, nor, I verily believe, anything more beautiful as an arrangement of colour--the huge wave, one sweep of blue, and the piece of gold at the top. It was, I was told, by an old master of Japan, and worth an enormous sum. The Japanese perfectly appreciate the value of things like that, and they very rarely let them leave the country, so that it has become very difficult to get hold of anything really fine.

An experience which gave me a close insight into Japanese feeling was a meeting of some of the painters of Japan. It was arranged by a Japanese gentleman who, though not an artist himself, is deeply interested in art, and keenly alive to everything touching it. Knowing me personally, he was anxious that I should come in contact with these men whose practice he so much revered, and so he invited several of these artists of different kinds--designers of metal work and designers for manufactures--to his house to meet me. I talked to them with his interpreting help, just a little about art and its principles and so forth, in the hope that the others would be brought to speak freely, and I expressed my readiness to give them what information I could of European art and its practice. They asked me remarkable questions. Most of them, it appeared, were discouraged because "the European required such ugly things." If they made what the Europeans really enjoyed, their productions were looked upon as unsaleable. It appeared to me that it must be extremely difficult for the Japs to hold fast to their artistic instincts, and in the end I expressed my conviction that it would pay them better to adhere to their principles rather than to pander to the foolish demands of the dull American or British merchant who had neither idea nor concern as to the beauty of the work he buys.

Unfortunately, to a great extent these traders are lowering the standard of painting in Japan. Not a few of these sixty men who came to meet me would do work they did not care about, not being men of such individuality and independence of character as Kiyosai. With them, as with us, the prize of money-reward is a bait too tempting to be resisted. Two days afterwards some of these friends were good enough to write a long discourse in one of the Japanese papers on my address, saying how much pleased they were to find an artist from England with my ideas of Japanese art--one who condemned the notion so common among them that it was necessary to pander to the tastes of a foreign market. They were especially glad that I had condemned that, and many of the painters, more or less on the strength of my conversation, decided to do thenceforth what they felt to be true to their principles--to go to nature and themselves, to choose their lovely harmony of colour, instead of designing stereotyped screens with gold birds on black backgrounds. Many were determined to give up that kind of art altogether, and one in particular (whose studio I called at the day after) pointed out that he had already quite altered his style. He was an artist by nature, and he told me he felt that having to do this horrible work was going against him, and he had made up his mind that in future he would insist upon doing what he felt to be beautiful, and would be ruled by the merchant no more. I visited the studios of a great many of the artists to whom I had delivered my lecture, and saw their sketch-books and their method of work. In nearly every case their method coincided with the principles laid down by Kiyosai--each having, of course, his own method, but each working in the same broad way of "impression picture."

Japan might be said to be as artistic as England is inartistic. In Japan art is not a cause, but a result--the result of the naturalness of the people--and is closely allied with all aspects of their daily life. In the houses, the streets, the gardens, the places of public resort--everywhere is to be found the all-pervading element of art and beauty. A rainy day in Japan is not, as it is in London, a day of gloom and horror, but a day of absolute fascination. What a joy is the spectacle of all those lovely yellow paper umbrellas unfurling themselves beneath a shower like flowers before the sun, so different from the dark shiny respectability of our ghastly gamps at home! John Bunyan has written and talked of the house beautiful; but the Japanese have given to the nation not only the house beautiful, but also (what is even more important to the community at large) the street beautiful, and that is where Japan differs so widely from Europe. As I walk through the London streets at night, how prosaic is the flicker of each gas-jet, within its sombre panes of glass, in some "long unlovely street," and how different from the softened rays that shine from out the dainty ricksha lanterns illuminating the streets in Japan! There a poem meets your eye with each step you take; and how pretty is every street corner, with its little shop, its mellow light and dainty arrangements, with the smiling face of some little child peeping out from the dim shadow beyond! It is a terrible thing to live in a country where art is the luxury of the few, and where the people know as little of what constitutes the beauty of life as a Hindoo knows of skating. What would a Japanese gentleman say, I wonder, if he passed into a room in the depths of winter and saw a quantity of those pretty fans, which in his country help to modify the heat of the golden summer days, viciously nailed, without rhyme or reason, upon a bright red wall, or those fairy-like umbrellas, upon which he has seen the rain-drops glisten so brightly, stuck within the gloomy recess of some lead-black hideous grate, or (with still less sense of the fitness of things or regard for the uses for which it was made) glued to a white-washed ceiling?

We sometimes talk of the deteriorating influence of European ideas upon Japanese art; but we have failed to perceive the ghastly inappropriateness of applying the Japs' delicate flights of fancy to our homes of discomfort. That usefulness is the basis of all righteousness is the moral code by which a man's position is gauged in Japan, and by which things are made. It does not matter how beautiful an article may be, or how trivial--whether it is a penholder, a snuff-box, or a pipe--if it is not useful it is considered inartistic, and will not be accepted by the Japanese public. The form of a vase or a cup, or the shape of a handle, must all be designed with a view to its usefulness; and every little work of art that is made, every cabinet and curio (apart from being decorative), is designed to convey some maxim-like idea, a lesson that will be useful and helpful in one way or another to the beholder.

On entering a Japanese tea-house you will see a kakemono hanging on the wall that strikes you at the first glance as being a perfect picture, with the bold but simple Chinese characters on the white silk and the tiny slip of vermilion which is the signature of the artist. It is placed well in the room, and is altogether a thing of beauty; but when, on closer inspection, you read the decorative letters, you will find that they give you some dainty piece of advice to help you through the day, or some pretty idea on which your eye and mind can rest.

Then, again, the games that the children play in the streets with sand or pebbles--they are teaching them arithmetic, construction, patience, and innumerable valuable lessons.

Usefulness is the basis of the ancient caste system of Japan, which system exists at the present day, and upon which the relative usefulness of a man depends. Take the Samurai. They occupy the premier position as Japanese aristocracy, because, although they wear silk, they give up their lives for their country--and no man can be more useful than that. The agriculturalist ranks next in dignity; for none can do without food, and therefore his usefulness is indisputable. Then come the workmen, and last of all the merchants, who are considered as "no class" in Japan and are greatly looked down upon--

producing nothing, they merely turn over articles made by other hands for a profit.

The most beautiful article we possess (one that is entirely our own) is the hansom cab. It is perhaps one of the greatest triumphs that the West has produced in the shape of a conveyance, and simply because it has been designed with a view to its usefulness. Would that we were always ruled by this splendid quality! Unfortunately, we are not. We are ruled by our own tastes, which, I feel bound to admit, are not artistic. Think of the sombre, happy-go-lucky arrangements of our London theatres. How is it that in the best-managed of them an actress will so far forget herself as to lie dying in the middle of a snowy street in the dead of night, pale-faced and wretched-looking, with ten thousand pounds' worth of jewellery on her fingers? Such a scene would drive the artistic and consistent Japanese manager into the nearest lunatic asylum. At the same time he would be unutterably shocked at seeing a red moon (red, let us trust, with the blush of shame at its creator's folly) rising hurriedly behind some stage bank of roses, swiftly and unnaturally hurrying across a purple sky, and shamefacedly setting in the East, in the West, in the North, in the South, within the brief hour of an English stage, as if glad to escape the rapturous applause of an inartistic public.

But perhaps nowhere is the difference between European and Japanese art so sharply accentuated as it is in the teaching of it in the great schools of the West and of the East. Let us take the art schools of Paris, which is considered by a vast portion of the artistic world to be the very paradise of art. You enter the crowded studio of some well-known master, and you see before you a large white statue, the first and predominant impression of which is its exceeding whiteness; and to your mingled amusement and amazement you discover that the unfortunate pupils are engaged in a futile endeavour to render an impression of exceeding whiteness by the aid of thick black chalk or charcoal. As to how this is to be done with any degree of verisimilitude you are no less at fault than they are, poor dears, themselves; and therefore you will not be surprised that, dazed and wearied as they must be from the steady contemplation of this never-ending pose, their work at the close of a day resembles the figure from which they have been drawing as closely as the work of Michael Angelo, or any of the great Japanese masters.

From the antique you pass to the life room. Here another shock awaits you. In the middle of the room stands a young girl, strapped up in the attitude of Atalanta of classic fable running her immortal race. These pupils are taught first of all to sketch the figure in the pose of running as a skeleton. When the hideous skeleton has been carefully and laboriously committed to paper, it is with equal care imbued with nerves and muscles and flesh. When all this is done, a light Grecian drapery is flung on her, regardless of the folds and movement that would eventually have resulted from the fluttering of the breeze, and, mind you, she is strapped up all the time. Then, when all is completed, the poor dear lady is expected to run her immortal race. Of course, by this time there is no action in the figure at all. Atalanta appears glued to the spot, and my only wonder is that she does not indignantly chase her unfortunate creators from the studio. On looking at these pictures the spectator would say that he never saw anything so absolutely unsuggestive of the breathless vigour and energy of a healthy young girl engaged in a rapid race as is indicated by the pitiful weariness of that poor strapped-up creature in front of them. Would it not be far better that these students should go out into the street, after the method of the Japs, and watch some girl as she runs and jumps in the bright sunshine, with a soft wind blowing her hair about her head and her gown about her limbs, and then come back, and, with a memory of the beautiful inspiriting scene still fresh in their minds, commit their impressions "hot and hot" upon the canvas before them?

Still, England has not always been so hopelessly inartistic. None would think of denying the perfect taste of the architects who designed such buildings as the Winchester and Durham Cathedrals, and Arundel Castle; but those are buildings wrought in dead days by men a long time dead, and England's days of artistic appreciation are, I fear, as dead as they are. Commerce and so-called civilisation have ruined us, I fear, for ever. Japan is as artistic to-day as we were five hundred years ago, and I rejoice to think that at present there appears to be little fear of so ghastly a fate as has overtaken us. As a nation the Japanese remain faithful to art in all its details, and as individuals they are still a nation of artists. Where else but in Japan would an aged gentleman dream of rising ere the day has well begun, merely that he might bring into harmony with all its surroundings, and present in the best light possible, a little flower placed in a pot--bending it this way and that way, that its attitude might conform with the cabinet in one corner of the room, or a screen in the other? Who but a Japanese chamber-boy would be so impressed with the artistic value of contrast merely that he would feel constrained thereby to place the can of hot water in a different attitude every time he brought it into the room, and thoughtfully step aside to regard its consonance with its immediate surroundings? Art begins, as charity begins, at home; and where the home of the individual is absolutely artistic, it cannot fail that the whole nation should be a nation of artists. I give way to none in my loyalty to my country and my love for that country--I must say that I do not think that there is a country better in the whole world;--but perfection on this earth is not only impossible, but to my idea also absolutely undesirable--a perfect nation would be to the full as dreadful as a perfect man. We are saved from perfection by an almost entire lack of the artistic faculty, and, however great we are in other respects, I am sad to say we are thoroughly inartistic. To whom but the Englishman would the golden dragons that play so recklessly about on black screens with their scarlet drooping tongues, that are sold in the Japanese curio shops, possibly appeal? Who but English-speaking people would crave for those cherry-blossoms embroidered on white silk grounds, which they so gleefully carry away with them? Who but my inartistic countrymen would insist on their cabinets being smothered with endless and miscellaneous carvings? The Japanese are too artistic to admit these things into their own homes; but why are their dealers so inartistic as (blinded by the desire of filthy pelf) to put forth these embroideries for the English and American market? Such things now and then make me tremble for the future of art in Japan. It may be (though I trust not) the thin end of the wedge; it may be "the little rift within the lute that by and by will make the music mute, and, ever widening, slowly silence all." What a tragedy it would be that the music of this most perfect art should ever be silenced in that lovely land, the resting-place and home of the highest and only living art!

CHAPTER III

PAINTERS AND THEIR METHODS

The methods of painters all over the world are very much alike. In fact, the methods of great masters (no matter of what nationality, and whether of this period or of centuries past) are often precisely similar, while there can be no doubt but that some of the finest masterpieces ever painted very closely resemble one another. I was once taken to see two photographs, one a portion of a figure by Michael Angelo, and the other a portion of a Japanese buddha by one of Japan's greatest masters; and to my surprise I found that it was almost impossible to detect which was which. This particular statue of Michael Angelo's I had studied and knew well; yet here was a portion of a Japanese god that looked exactly the same--the same broad handling, the same everything. In both there was the same curious exaggeration of the bones and muscles, wrong from the anatomical standpoint, yet conveying an impression of terrific strength that is so typical of the work of Michael Angelo--indeed, one masterly hand might have executed both pictures. Yet the little Japanese artist, the creator of this Buddha, was but a modern, and in all probability had never so much as seen Michael Angelo's pictures, much less had he been in the slightest degree influenced by him.

Japanese painters have a great admiration for Michael Angelo's work, and for Italian painters in general. If you were to show a Japanese artist, any ordinary little minor artist, some photographs of masterpieces by men such as Velasquez, Rembrandt, and Botticelli, you would find that he would at once spring on to the early Italian work, peer into it, hold it up, devour it, muttering to himself the while--nothing could tear him away. Rembrandt does not appeal to him much; Velasquez not much; but Botticelli--yes. Still, I have often thought that could Hokusai and Velasquez, Kiosi and Whistler, have met and talked, they would have had much in common with one another; for there is in the works of each, although in many senses so widely different, that simplicity, truthfulness, and restraint which render them all so very much alike.

The broad principles of art are much the same all the world over; but it is between the lesser artists of Japan and the myriads of comparatively unknown artists of Europe that there is so great a gulf fixed. Japanese minor artists are artists indeed. Our minor artists are, I fear, anything but artists. The veriest Japanese craftsman is an artist first and a tradesman afterwards. Ours is a tradesman first and last and altogether; and even as a tradesman he is, I fear, a failure, for the honest tradesman has at least something worth the selling, whilst our men--the jerry builder, the plumber, the furniture maker, and the carpenter--give in return for solid money an article which it would break the heart of the merest artisan in Japan to put forward as the work of his hands. But perhaps nowhere is the difference between European and Japanese art so sharply accentuated as it is in the teaching of it in the great schools of the East and of the West. We Westerners are taught to draw direct from the object or model before us on the platform, whereas the Japanese are taught to study every detail of their model, and to store their brains with impressions of every curve and line, afterwards to go away and draw that object from memory. This is a splendid training for the memory and the eye, as it teaches one both to see and to remember--two great considerations in the art of drawing. You will often see a little child sitting in a garden in Japan gazing attentively for perhaps a whole hour at a bowl of goldfish, watching the tiny bright creatures as they circle round and round in the bowl. Remarking on some particular pose, the child will retain it in its busy brain, and, running away, will put down this impression as nearly as it can remember. Perhaps on this first occasion he is only able to put in a few leading lines; very soon he is at a loss--he has forgotten the curve of the tail or the placing of the eye. He toddles back and studies the fish again and again, until perhaps after one week's practice that child is able to draw the fish in two or three different poses from memory without the slightest hesitation or uncertainty.

It is this certainty of touch and their power to execute these bold, sweeping, decided lines that form the chief attraction of Japanese works of art. Their wrists are supple; the picture in their minds is sure; they have learnt it line for line; it is merely the matter of a few minutes for an artist to sketch in his picture. There are no choppy hesitating lines such as one detects in even the finest of our Western pictures, lines in which you can plainly see how the artist has swerved first to the right and then to the left, correcting and erasing, uncertain in his touch. The lines will probably be correct in the end; but when the picture is finished his work has not that bright crisp look so characteristic of the Japanese pictures. Then, again, when a Japanese artist draws a bird, he begins with the point of interest--which, let us say, is the eye. The brilliant black eye of a crow fixed upon a piece of meat attracts his attention; he remembers it, and the first few strokes that he portrays upon his stretched silk is the eye of the bird. The neck, the legs, the body-- everything radiates and springs from that bright eye just as it does in the animal itself.

Then, again, let us say a Japanese artist is painting a typical Japanese river-scene, such a one as inspired many of Mr. Whistler's graceful Thames etchings--a quaintly formed bridge under whose dim archway a glimpse of shipping and masses of detail can be seen in the distance. To a Japanese artist the chief charm and interest of such a scene would lie in that little view beneath the bridge, and he would begin by drawing in, line for line, every little mast and funnel just as he sees it, or rather as he remembers it. The picture slowly expands as it reaches the margin, ending in the bridge, which forms, as it were, a frame through which to view the dainty richness of detail of the busy scene beyond. If you were to arrest this picture at any moment during its career you would find that it formed a perfect whole, every line balancing the other; whereas, according to our methods, if we were to draw the bridge first, timidly suggesting the distance and leaving the detail and all the fine lines to be put in afterwards, as so many artists do, the picture until it was completed would appear spotty and uneven. And even when finished there would be no balance, for we neither understand nor realise the importance of that quality without which no work of art can be perfect.

The Japanese methods of drawing and painting are entirely opposed to our Western methods, and in order to give a slight insight into the works of the Japanese painters I must describe these methods as minutely and as clearly as is possible. To begin with, the size of an ordinary picture is two feet by four and a half long, and as a rule three times as much space is left at the top as at the bottom of the picture. The brushes consist of a series of round ones; they are flat-ended and vary greatly in breadth, being named after the character of work they are fitted for. Straw brushes are sometimes used for coarse work. The silk that they paint upon is prepared in the following manner. First the edges of the wooden frame are pasted and the silk is rolled loosely over, great care being taken to keep the grain of the silk level. The surface of the silk is prepared with alum and size, the proportion of which is about an egg-spoonful of alum to a small tea-cupful of size. The size is boiled and strained and diluted with water, and the alum is added over the fire; it is again strained, and is then ready for use. Finally, it is put on to the surface while hot with a large brush. It is usual to put on two coats, and a contrivance in the shape of a cross piece of wood at the back of the frame is used for straining the silk more tightly after the first coat of size. The colours that the Japanese use are mixed and prepared in the following manner. Whitening, which is the basis of most colours, is pounded with a pestle and mortar into a very fine powder; then a little size which has been boiled and strained is poured in, and the whole is beaten up and worked into a ball. This ball is thrown over and over again into the mortar until it is well beaten. A little water is poured over the lump, which is then heated over a fire until it breaks and spreads. In this state, after cooling a little, it is well worked up, with perhaps the addition of water, until a white pulpy putty is produced; the artist is very careful all the time to avoid grit. Other colours are principally prepared from powders, which are beaten up in little porcelain cups with small pestles, and are mixed with a little size and water into saucers, stirred all the while with the finger and heated over the fire until dry, or nearly so. When required for use they must be worked up again with the finger and water, and it is a good plan when first mixing the colours to paste paper over the saucers, leaving a small hole for the insertion of the brush. Gamboge and a vegetable red resembling crimson lake are both used without size. The latter is prepared from a woollen material which is torn up into shreds and put into a saucer; then it is mixed with boiling water and afterwards strained through paper. It is drawn off in small quantities into several saucers and carefully dried over the fire. There is a colour which is much used called Taisha, which is like burnt sienna; then there is Tan, a sort of orange, and Shi, a vermilion red. The red is prepared in two different ways, first by being mixed cold in a cup with a pestle, a little size, and water. In this preparation the colour separates into a deep red and orange, the latter floating on the top. The orange is afterwards saved and used instead of Tan--Tan, not being permanent, turns black and disappears; it is used sometimes to shade ladies' faces, but fades very much. In using this preparation of orange and red, the brush must be first dipped in yellow and then the tip of it in the red, so as to take up both portions of the mixture.

Another way of preparing Shi is to heat a saucer until the finger can hardly bear the touch, and then pour in some size and put the powdered pigment in it while still on the fire. When it has dried it is taken off and mixed with the finger very hot, a little water being added gradually, until it is of a thickish consistency. Shi thus mixed is of a deep red without any orange precipitate, and is used for upper washes, for, having a great deal of orange in it, it would be too black if used for undertones. In mixing indigo blue from a cake, the saucer is put over the fire to dry, and a little size is added. It is then rubbed with the finger, and water is gradually added. Taisha, when in a cake, is also prepared in this way. Taisha is used for the face and hair. The hair is shaded off with Indian ink, and the muscles of the face are washed in with Taisha having no white but a little black mixed with it; the feet and hands are handled in the same way. Then the face is washed over again with the same colour, only a little lighter. Broad masses of shading are introduced, and the nose, mouth, and edge of the cheek are generally left to be shaded in. It is considered better to use a number of light tones than one dark tone, and the washes on the face are repeated two or three times. The hair also is washed over with a large brush and rather dark ink; the eyebrows are put in in a single wash; also the corners of the eyes and mouth, which are flicked in and then washed off again. The lips are put in with vermilion and shaded off with another brush. A mixture of red, white, and Indian ink forming a dull purple is used for the pupils of the eyes, and the same mixture with a greater proportion of red, and consequently a little lighter, is used for going over the outline, and the ends of some of the lines are washed off with another brush. The same purple colour, but lighter still, is used as a backing to the outline in order to soften the edges, and a few touches of purple are painted in under the eyes and ears. The lips are touched with carmine, and the teeth and eyeballs with a little white. The under-lip and corners of the eyes are touched with lines or dots of light Indian ink, and the top eyelids and tops of lower eyelids are outlined with thin lines. The outline of the pupil is very fine; but the dot of the eye is made very black; the nostrils are painted in in light ink, shaded off afterwards and outlined in black. The hair round the mouth is put in in very light ink with a finely pointed brush.

There are many ways of painting the hair. Sometimes a fine brush is used with single parallel lines, and sometimes it is washed in with a broad brush with light ink below and darker above. In old silk pictures great depth used to be obtained by painting the hair on the back of the silk as well as on the front. For painting leaves a mixture of indigo and gamboge is generally used with a full brush, the tip of the brush being dipped in indigo. By this method, the dark colour on the tip of the brush being after a time exhausted, the lighter green appears, and thus a natural variety of gradation is given to the colour of the leaves. Trees and rocks, etc., are often scrubbed in with a rather dry brush worked sideways and forming broken lines.

Another method of drawing a figure is to outline in charcoal, after which the face with its markings is outlined with a kind of Indian ink. Then with the same Indian ink, but with broader lines and a large brush, the drapery is boldly swept in with lines that should break in parts and form a drag. This drag must come naturally by pressing the brush firmly on the silk or paper; any attempt to force it would end in failure. The hair should then be worked in with a large spread brush, care being taken to give the hairs a radial tendency and not let them cross confusedly. Sometimes this hair is painted with a fine brush and with single lines. For the background two large brushes are used, one fitted with light ink and the other with plain water to shade off the black. The face and the breast are treated in the same way. The outlines of the drapery are sometimes washed in with a lighter tone to project over the edge and soften them. The face is washed with a mixture of red and ink, leaving only the eyes. The work is finished by using a small brush and very black ink for the markings of the mouth, centre of the eyes, under the eyelids, nostrils, and ear-rings.

Japanese artists study a great deal from life, and in order to draw a figure full of spirit and action they will often work in this way. Beginning with a very full brush, they sketch in the general swing of the figure with a few well-chosen broad black lines--as, for instance, when drawing the legs of a horse or a lobster they will put them in with one broad wash. Then they strain thin Japanese paper over this spirited sketch, and begin to elaborate on it with finer work, until in the end they produce a picture that has high finish, but possessing all the action and spirit of a first impression.

The Japanese system of studying Nature in detail, but not with a view to creating a picture, is perhaps especially noticeable in their drawings of women. It would be considered coarse and vulgar in the extreme to paint a woman in the glaring light of a studio, copying every feature and wrinkle, line for line, as you would copy a man. Kiyosai explains that it is impossible to create a beautiful face by drawing direct from life, especially in line. The only way in which it can be achieved is by suggesting a natural beauty on paper, and by imitating a conventional type away from nature. The Japanese have a conventional type of beauty just as we have, and just as the Greeks had years ago--an ideal that has been evolved from the aggregate of myriads of beautiful women,--and this ideal of theirs must be a woman possessing small lips, with eyelids scarcely showing, and eyebrows far above the eyes. The forehead must be narrow at the top and widening towards the base, looking altogether very like a pyramid with its top cut off; the nose should be aquiline, and the whole woman must appear to be the personification of softness and delicacy. The conventional type of a Japanese man has always the legs and arms placed in impossible positions to denote strength, and the muscles are greatly exaggerated.

In the old masters of Japan great importance is attached to flesh markings, more especially in pictures of men. In a sketch of a fat man trying to lift a heavy weight, the action would be suggested in a few swift lines with no shading, but just two small horizontal lines at the back of the neck. Those two little flesh markings portray the fat man to perfection, admirably suggesting both the strain of the action and the bulk of the man. But in talking of the art of Japan and the methods of the Japanese painter, I feel that I cannot do better than describe a day that I once spent with that greatest of all living artists, Kiyosai, at the house of Captain Brinkley. This gentleman invited Kiyosai to come to his house one morning, and I was asked to watch and follow the whole process of his work, and as far as possible to learn from him his theories about painting. It was a splendid chance for me as a painter, especially as Captain Brinkley, who has resided in Japan for many years, and is a Japanese scholar of high attainment, acted as interpreter between Kiyosai and myself.

Kiyosai, I may say, is known all over Japan. From the highest noble to the lowest ragged child in the streets, all know the artist and love his work, for the pictures of a popular painter get abroad in Japan much as they get abroad here--Kiyosai's pictures and sketches being reproduced and published in the Japanese papers just as they would be published in Western magazines. When any drawing by Kiyosai appears a rush is made for the paper. These drawings of his are really superb work, and I could not help feeling how great a privilege it was to come into contact with such a man.

I arrived at my host's quite early in the morning, for I was to have a whole day with my Japanese fellow-worker. I was introduced at once to an old man, grave and very dignified in bearing, and I found it difficult at first to realise that this was the painter of whom I had heard so much. He was sitting on the floor smoking, while his assistant was busy stretching silk and preparing colours. As a rule, to see a Japanese smoke is to get at once a clue to the nature of the people. But Kiyosai was peculiar even in this. He was one of the few men who would take only one draw from his pipe; in the most dignified manner possible he would take that one whiff and then knock out the contents of his pipe, repeating the process as long as he continued to smoke. He had the most remarkable hands, too, ever seen, with long and slim thumbs--more sensitive, artistic, capable hands, from the chiromancer's point of view, could hardly be. He was enthusiastic, but prodigiously dignified, and used his hands just a little, yet in the most impressive way. He never rose from his sitting posture, and every time I said anything that was at all complimentary he received it with charming ceremony, by bowing to the very ground.

No sooner was I introduced than his face seemed to light up, his eyes became intensely brilliant, and his conversation not less so. He was enthusiastic in his desire to learn about English painters and English art generally, and eager to tell me his own views of art, and all he felt about it. To my pleased confusion, he seemed to regard me with an interest equalling mine for him. He put many questions about English art, and told me much that was interesting about his own. He spoke of the effect made on him by some English pictures. "I have seen a number of English and European pictures," he said; "but they all appear to me very much alike. I hear that in England and all over Europe they say the Japanese pictures look to them all alike. Why is this?" The explanation was not immediately forthcoming, for at first sight it seemed so extraordinary that to this man English pictures looked all alike. But immediately the truth forced itself upon me, as it will force itself upon the reader. European pictures are all wonderfully alike. It struck me that when, not long before, I was on a "hanging committee," and had passing before me several thousand pictures, it was only here and there that my attention was arrested by the individuality of some of the work. For the most part they were the same pigments, the same high lights, and the same deep shadows; and mentally seeing this procession of pictures pass before me, I could not avoid seeing how grievously alike European pictures were. I had in some sort, indeed, felt this before, and was delighted on having the impression "fixed," so to speak, by the Japanese master.

I saw a number of Japanese pictures, and I certainly found them far more individual than our work is. We say these Japanese works are insipid, out of perspective, and all pretty much the same. Here is a painter of Japan who brings a similar charge against our much more complex pictures--this, surely, is a new and a valuable lesson, full of suggestion for the thoughtful painter!

Kiyosai next began to discuss drawing, and, as he was speaking to an Englishman, English drawing in particular. "I hear that when artists in England are painting," he said, "if they are painting a bird, they stand that bird up in their back garden, or in their studio, and begin to paint it at once, then and there, never quite deciding what they are going to paint, never thinking of the particular pose and action of the bird that is to be represented on the canvas. Now, suppose that bird suddenly moves one leg up--what does the English artist do then?" He could not understand how an English painter could paint with the model before him. I naturally told him that they copied what they saw; that they got over the difficulty as best they could. "I do not quite understand that," he said. "In my own practice I look at the bird; I want to paint him as he is. He has got a pose. Good! Then he suddenly puts down his head, and there is another pose. The bare fact of the bird being there in an altered pose would compel me to alter my idea; and so on, until at last I could paint nothing at all." I asked him what, then, was his method. "I watch my bird," he replied, "and the particular pose I wish to copy before I attempt to represent it. I observe that very closely until he moves and the attitude is altered. Then I go away and record as much of that particular pose as I can remember. Perhaps I may be able to put down only three or four lines; but directly I have lost the impression I stop. Then I go back again and study that bird until it takes the same position as before. And then I again try and retain as much as I can of it. In this way I began by spending a whole day in a garden watching a bird and its particular attitude, and in the end I have remembered the pose so well, by continually trying to represent it, that I am able to repeat it entirely from my impression--but not from the bird. It is a hindrance to have the model before me when I have a mental note of the pose. What I do is a painting from memory, and it is a true impression. I have filled hundreds of sketch-books," he continued, "of different sorts of birds and fish and other things, and have at last got a facility, and have trained my memory to such an extent, that by observing the rapid action of a bird I can nearly always retain and produce it. By a lifelong training I have made my memory so keen that I think I may say I can reproduce anything I have once seen."

Such, then, is Kiyosai's method of work. It is purely natural, and one that has obtained for generations, and that is the Japanese whole theory of art. Captain Brinkley told me a story, the outcome of that conversation. Kiyosai came one day to work at a screen which Captain Brinkley was very anxious for him to complete; but he could not finish it at the time, do what he would. He said nothing; but it came out that he had a fresh impression in his mind, and he could not go on with the old impression until he had worked off the new one--something he had seen on his way up to the house.

The painters always live with fish, and birds, and animals of different sorts. They have fish in bottles and in ponds in their gardens. I went to many studios in Japan, and I found each one with its ponds and fish in the little garden surrounding the studio, and birds as well. They always study nature, and I believe that is the keynote of their art.

The technique of Kiyosai's work was most fascinating. I had come away from England with all sorts of theories concerning the technical part of an artist's work, and when I got to Japan I found there was absolutely nothing that was not known to this man. His method of work, too, interested me exceedingly. To begin with, the assistant brought his stretcher of silk--a lovely piece of silk stretched across a wooden frame--and placed it in front of him. Then, taking a long burnt twig, he thought for a few minutes, looking all the while at his silk--thought out his picture, indeed, before he put a single touch on his canvas. How different is this from the man who so often, with us, puts on a lot of hasty touches in the hope that they will suggest the picture! When this artist saw his picture complete in his mind, he began with the little burnt twig to trace a few sure lines. I never saw such facility in my life. A few swift strokes indicated the outline on the silk of two black crows; then he took up his brush and began at once with the Indian ink, with full powerful colour; and in about seven minutes he had completed a picture, superbly drawn and full of character--a complete impression of two black crows, very nearly life-size, resting on the branch of a tree.

Kiyosai never amid any circumstances repeats himself: every picture he paints is different, while for his work he asks but a small price. After he had done his crows he painted a coloured picture, beginning with Indian ink. First he tried all his colours, which were ready prepared in different little blue pots and placed around him. These little shallow pots or saucers had each its own liquid, which the assistant had prepared to a certain extent beforehand. They contained flesh tint, drapery colour, tones for hair, gold ornaments, and so forth. These colours had evidently been used before, as they were in their saucers, merely requiring dilution before immediate use. The saucers were arranged chiefly on his right, with a great vessel of water, of which he used a great deal. All his utensils were scrupulously clean. When he began there was no fishing for tones as on the average palette. No accident! All was sure--a scientific certainty from beginning to the end. The picture was the portrait of a woman. It displayed enormous facility and great knowledge, and his treatment of the drapery was remarkable; but altogether it pleased me less. No attempt was there at what is called broken colour. A black dress would be one beautiful tone of black, and flesh one clean tone of flesh, shadows growing out of the mass and forming a part of the whole. As this work was a very simple impression, he finished the coloured picture in a few minutes. But on the whole, in one sense, it was less satisfactory. It appeared as if he had studied his subject less, for it was a little conventional. He was less happy in it; but, of course, he did not admit this to himself.

He did four pictures, and each of them took from about seven to ten minutes, these constituting the finest lesson in water-colour painting I ever received in my life. Here is his idea of finish: once the impression of the detail and the finish of the object is recorded you can do nothing better; so far as the painter's impression of finish goes, so far must the rendering go, and no farther. Artistically he had become exhausted by doing these four pictures--in invention, I mean. You see, the man was heart and soul in the work. He lives, poor fellow, on almost nothing. He is a very independent man, refusing to work for money, and declining to paint for the market.

Nearly every artist in Japan has his own favourite stick of Indian ink, which he values as his very life. It is essential that this ink should be of the very finest quality, for they drink so much of it. In order to execute those fine lines ending in a broad sweep that is so characteristic of Japanese pictures, an artist must first fill his brush with Indian ink and then apply it to his lips until the tip becomes pointed. The ink is of course swallowed; but if it is of a good quality, to drink pints of it would not do a man the slightest harm. A practical proof of this can be found in the fact that Kiyosai, who is an old man, has been drinking Indian ink steadily with every picture he has painted all through his lifetime. He possesses a small piece of Indian ink which is hundreds of years old, and which all the money in the world could not buy. It is far too precious for broad washes, and is only used here and there for bright touches.

I noticed the tender way in which Kiyosai handled this one precious piece of Indian ink, and that led to a very interesting conversation on blacks, after which I realised that the variations and gradations to be procured with black alone were enormous. Kiyosai told me that when he was very young he was puzzled by the exceedingly rich quality of black in one of his master's pictures. It was a deep, velvety, luminous black, and young Kiyosai struggled for weeks and weeks to match it, but in vain. He came to the conclusion that there must be some work going on at the back of the picture, and at last one night he became so desperate that, stealing into his master's room while he lay asleep, he soaked off the picture which had been pasted on to a board, and looked at the back of it. One glance was enough, and little Kiyosai, with a throb of pleasure, hastily pasted the picture together again and stole away to experiment all that night on silk and on paper, "painting black both on the front and on the back."

I inquired of Kiyosai if he had ever painted in oils, and he assured me that he had not; but a few days later Captain Brinkley showed me a little picture painted in lacquer by Kiyosai which, in my opinion, rivalled for brilliancy any oil picture that has ever been painted, or has still to be painted. The surface was as brilliant as glass; yet the picture had a depth which no ordinary oil pigment could hope to reach, while its deep luminous shadows would put to shame the finest of Van Eyck's pictures.

An English friend of mine resident in Japan once told me a story of Kiyosai which struck me as being typical of that great master. A friend of his had prepared four magnificent sliding panels covered with the finest silk, and had given them to the painter with the request that he would execute some of his masterpieces on them for him. For eight or nine years Kiyosai had kept those panels, and they still remained bare; but great masters are always erratic, and the would-be purchaser never gave up hope. One day, however, he burst in upon my friend with the terrible intelligence that Kiyosai was dead drunk and had ruined his panels. "He's smashing away at them on the floor, and he is simply crawling over them," he said in a towering rage. My friend agreed to go round with him to Kiyosai's house to try if possible to stop the outrage. When they arrived they found the master in a high state of fever, and looking more like a wild animal than a human being, with his tusk-like teeth and his poor pitted face, sweeping and hacking about all over the silken panels. As they entered, Kiyosai left the room, leaving behind him the panels scattered irregularly over the floor, but each one smothered with work. "Look here," said my friend very generously: "it was I that introduced Kiyosai to you, and it was I that suggested his painting these doors; therefore it is only fair that I should relieve you of them and find you a new set, which I will willingly do." But the owner of the panels, shrewdly guessing that my friend had not made this magnanimous offer without some good reason, changed his mind and said that he could on no account receive so costly a gift. He kept them, and wisely too, for these four panels are now universally considered as some of Kiyosai's greatest masterpieces.

Strange to say, Kiyosai, when painting his finest work, is nearly always drunk, and his weakness is often taken a mean advantage of by the people around him. I remember once attending a party given by a Legation person who had invited a dozen or so of Japan's finest artists--among them the great Kiyosai, the master--to paint pictures on the floor for the edification of the assembled guests--a rather vulgar proceeding. Kiyosai resented this indignity with all the force of his passionate nature, but out of kindness allowed himself to be over-persuaded by his host. They made him drink and keep on drinking to build up his enthusiasm; but, boiling over with rage and indignation, he kept on putting off his time until the whole twelve artists had finished the sketches, although, fearing that the effect of the drink would wear off, the guests begged him to start at once. At last Kiyosai's time came. The silk lay prepared on the floor, with the ink and brushes ready for him to begin. Mad with rage and hating his unsympathetic audience, Kiyosai stood, or rather knelt, before his silk, fiercely grasping the brush, holding it downwards with all his fingers round it and thumb turned outwards. He looked like a god as he knelt there, gripping his brush and staring at the silk--he was seeing his picture. He executed a flight of crows, a masterpiece--Kiyosai knew it was a masterpiece--and, proudly drawing himself up to his full height, quivering in every limb, he threw down his brush, skidded the silk along the floor towards the spectators, and, saying "That is Kiyosai," left the house in disgust. The dignity of the little man cowed his spectators. Every one unconsciously felt the magnetism of the man, and realised that a master had been among them.

PLACING

CHAPTER IV

PLACING

In Japan there is no such thing as accident. A scene which in its beauty and perfect placing appears to the visitor to be the result of Nature in an unusually generous mood, has in reality been the object of infinite care and thought and anxious deliberation to these little Japanese artists, the landscape gardeners. That temple which seems to place itself so remarkably well in relation to the big lines of Nature, its background, has been carefully built and thought out from that standpoint alone. The great trees by the side of the temple, with their graceful jutting boughs that form the principal feature of the picture, have not grown like that, for all their apparent naturalness; they have been nursed and grafted and forced into shape with the utmost care imaginable.

The sense of perfect placing, which is the sense of balance, is the true secret of the Japanese art, by which they attain perfection. All Orientals are more or less possessed of this intuitive sense of balance, and the Japanese carry it into the most minute details of daily life. If you enter a Japanese room you will always find that the bough of blossom is placed in relation to the kakemono and other furniture to form a picture. And the special note of Japanese house decoration is this bough of blossom, with which I was immensely struck. Now, this is an altogether artistic thing. At one party at which I was present I saw a piece of blossom-bough put right out at a curious angle from a beautiful blue jar. Turning to my neighbour, a young Japanese friend who could talk English perfectly well, I said, "How beautiful that is!--although, of course, its quaint curious form is merely accident." "No--no accident at all," he replied. "Do you know, it has been a matter of great care, this placing of the plant in the room in relation to other objects?"--I was afterwards informed that in many a household in Japan the children are trained in the method of placing a branch or a piece of blossom, and they have books with diagrams illustrating the proper way of disposing flowers in a pot.

The outsides as well as the insides of their houses are decorated in the harmonious principle, even to the painting of signs in the street. They are most particular about placing their richly coloured sign duly in relation to its surroundings. In the same way--whether the subject may be done in a string of lanterns or what not--whatever is done is done harmoniously, and in no case is decoration the result of accident. The sum of it all is that every shop in an ordinary street is a perfect picture. At first you are amazed at the beauty of everything. "How in the world is it," you ask yourself, "that by a series of apparent accidents everything appears beautiful?" You cannot imagine until you know that even the "common man" has acquired the scientific placing of his things, and that the feeling permeates all classes. Perhaps, however, one of the most curious experiences I had of the native artistic instinct of Japan occurred in this way I had got a number of fanholders and was busying myself one afternoon in arranging them upon the walls. My little Japanese servant boy was in the room, and as I went on with my work I caught an expression on his face from time to time which showed that he was not over-pleased with my performance. After a while, as this dissatisfied expression seemed to deepen, I asked him what the matter was. Then he frankly confessed that he did not like the way in which I was arranging my fanholders. "Why did you not tell me so at once?" I asked. "You are an artist from England," he replied, "and it was not for me to speak." However, I persuaded him to arrange the fanholders himself after his own taste, and I must say that I received a remarkable lesson. The task took him about two hours, placing, arranging, adjusting; and when he had finished the result was simply beautiful. That wall was a perfect picture; every fanholder seemed to be exactly in its right place, and it looked as if the alteration of a single one would affect and disintegrate the whole scheme. I accepted the lesson with due humility, and remained more than ever convinced that the Japanese are what they have justly claimed to be, an essentially artistic people instinct with living art.

It is, in point of fact, almost impossible to exaggerate the importance attached to the placing of an object by every Japanese, and it would be no exaggeration to say that if a common coolie were given an addressed envelope to stamp he would take great pains to place that little coloured patch in relation to the name and address in order to form a decorative pattern. Can you imagine a tradesman and his family, wife and children, running across the Strand to watch the placing of a saucepan in their window? Yet this is no unusual occurrence in Japan. You will often see a family collected on the opposite side of the road watching their father place a signboard in front of his shop. It might be a grocer's shop, and all--even to the mite strapped to the back of its sister--are eagerly watching the moving about of this board, and are interested to see that it should place itself well in relation to the broad masses around, such as the tea-box, etc.

Now, people who think so much of the details of balance must necessarily approach art in a very different manner from that in which we approach it. Would a tradesman in England hesitate before placing his stamps on a bill? The tradesman in Japan does. Imagine an artist spending three days in anxious thought as to where he should place his signature on his picture! And yet this is what Kiyosai, the greatest of modern painters, actually did before he affixed his red stamp to the hasty sketch of a crow. I have known little Japanese painters to ponder for hours, and sometimes weeks, over the placing of this little vermilion stamp so that it shall form perfect balance, and in all probability the picture itself has only taken a few minutes. Suppose, for instance, a painter has contrived to produce a rapid sketch of a flying crow, or perhaps a fish. That fleeting impression was so strong that he was able to produce it at once without any hesitation; but however vivid and lifelike the picture might be, if the balance were destroyed by the ugly placing of this one little spot of vermilion, from the Japanese standpoint the picture would be utterly worthless. And the proper placing of a thing is really most important. Even the most ignorant and uneducated in matters of art are influenced on seeing a perfect bit of placing. To live with some beautiful thing, a flower or a bough well placed, to watch its delicious curves or the tender buds of a purple iris just bursting, must give joy, and it does, although one may be quite unconscious of its gentle power.

The Japanese understand these subtleties as do no other nation. If they are entertaining a guest, their one aim and object is to make him perfectly and deliriously happy; they strive to divine his inmost thoughts and desires; it is their ambition to satisfy them to the best of their ability.

A friend of mine, an American, once gave me a description of a week he had spent with a very ancient Japanese gentleman in a little country village; it was a week of intense interest and happiness to him, one which, when he grows to be as old as his host was then, will still remain in his memory with a lingering sweetness as something good to be remembered, something purer and quite apart from the regular routine of his past life. He was a student, a naturalist; and the purity of this Japanese household, the seclusion and dainty decoration of his study, the freedom of it all, and the kindly attention and sympathy that was proffered to him by every member of the family combined to make the quiet recluse feel, for once in his life, almost boisterously happy. Towards the end of his visit he tried to look back and discover what it was that had brought about this unwonted feeling of joy in him, little realising that all this time these dear people had been scheming and planning for no other object than to give him pleasure. It was not until the last day of his stay, however, that it all unfolded itself clearly before his eyes, and that he learnt the reason why he had been so happy. On this last morning he had chanced to rise early--at daybreak, in fact--and as he passed the room that he had been using as a general sitting-room, he saw through the partially-opened sliding doors a sight which caught his breath with amazement, and made tears spring to his eyes. There was his host, the dear ancient Japanese gentleman, kneeling before a bough of pink blossom, which he was struggling to arrange in a fine blue china pot. The naturalist stood and watched him for nearly an hour, as he clipped a bough here, and bent a twig there, leaning back on his heels now and then to view his handiwork through half-closed eyes. He must see that the blossom placed itself well from the decorative standpoint in relation to the kakemono that hung close by; he must also see that the curves of the bough were correct; and the care taken by this old gentleman in the bending of the bough was a lesson to my friend. It became clear to him that every morning his aged host must have risen at daybreak to perform this little act of kindness. Like a flash he remembered that each day there had been some dainty new arrangement of flowers placed in his room for him to enjoy. He had not given it much thought, for it looked more or less like an accident, flowers that had formed themselves naturally into that shape; yet, all unconsciously, this little bit of perfect placing had influenced his work and had gone far towards making the visit so joyous to him. He did not understand placing; but it interested him and gave him an intense amount of pleasure, in the same way that superbly fine work always does even to the most uneducated.

The proper placing of objects is not only an exact science, but also it forms almost a religion with the Japanese. When you just arrive in Japan you are at once impressed with the perfect placing of everything about you. You find yourself surrounded by a series of beautiful pictures; every street that you see on your journey from the station to the hotel is a picture; every shop front, the combination of the many streets, the town in relation to the mountains round about it--everything you chance to look at forms a picture. In fact, the whole of Japan is one perfect bit of placing.

"Nature has favoured this place," says the globe-trotter. "I never found when I lived in Surrey that great trees placed themselves against hill-sides so as to form perfect pictures. I never saw the lines of a bush pick up those of a fence with one broad sweep. Nature never behaved like that in Dorking." Of course Nature didn't; nor does she in Japan. There the whole country, every square inch of it, is thought out and handled by great artists. There is no accident in the beautiful curves of the trees that the globe-trotter so justly admires: these trees have been trained and shaped and forced to form a certain decorative pattern, and the result is--perfection. We in the West labour under the delusion that if Nature were to be allowed to have her own sweet way, she would always be beautiful. But the Japanese have gone much further than this: they realise that Nature does not always do the right thing; they know that occasionally trees will grow up to form ugly lines; and they know exactly how to adapt and help her. She is to them like some beautiful musical instrument, finer than any ever made by human hands, but still an instrument, with harmonies to be coaxed out. And the Japanese play on Nature, not only in a concentrated way as with a kakemono or a flower in a room, but also in the biggest possible form, on landscapes; dragging in mountains, colossal trees, rushing cataracts--nothing is too much or too great an undertaking for these masters of decoration. Any ordinary little baby boy that is born in Japan has almost a greater decorative sense than the finest painter here in the West.

All this beauty and perfection that meets one on every side is the result of centuries and centuries of habit, until it has become intuitive to the people. I can safely say there is no point in Japan where an artist cannot stand still and frame between his hands a picture that will be perfect in placing and design. In a Japanese garden, every stepping-stone, every tree, every little miniature out-house, is thought out as a bit of placing to form perfect balance. And it is thought out not as an isolated bit of Nature, but in relation to everything around that you can see, whether it is a temple, a large tree, or the side of a hill; and whatever position you happen to be in, in that garden you will always see a perfectly balanced picture. When you have been pottering about in the towns for some weeks, you eventually become accustomed to the idea that everything is thought out by these brilliant students in order to form a picture, and you begin to feel proud of the knowledge you have gleaned and to make practical use of it. You escort your friends, who are a trifle fresher than yourself, about the towns, pointing out to them that there is no accident in all the beauties that they so much admire--the shops, the signboards, the placing of the flower by the side of the workman--all this has been carefully thought out from the decorative standpoint, to be beautiful. But then, when one travels from the beaten track, away out in the country, even the resident who is by way of being artistic, and has had the fact that the Japanese are an artistic people driven into his stupid head by sheer force, even this poor dear is swept off his feet when he finds that Nature is still going on doing the same thing all these miles away from the town. He has probably come to view the cherry-blossom, and he discovers to his amazement that these huge hill-sides of blossom place themselves perfectly one against the other--colossal trees with jutty boughs frame themselves against the sides of the mountains to form a picture. One huge sweep of blossom is thought out in relation to another sweep that is deeper in tone; near by is a curiously-shaped bare patch of earth which is designed to give value to the brighter colour; and so it continues indefinitely.

The whole country is thought out in huge blotches to form a picture perfect in harmony and in design. I once had a very interesting experience of the felling of a tree in Japan, and here again placing formed a very prominent part of the proceedings. Of course this was placing of a nature very different from the artistic placing that I have just described; but as a scientific bit of work it was simply wonderful! It was an enormous tree by the side of a temple; there were two little men sawing away at its base, little mites of men, half hidden by the huge gaping crowd, chiefly composed of children, that stood watching the performance, waiting for the tree to fall. A wall stood close by with an opening cut in it, just large enough to allow the trunk to place itself; and away in the distance strewn about at different angles were a series of huge stone boulders, and these, I soon found out, were to split up the boughs for firewood when the tree fell, thus saving labour. Imagine the science of it--the calculation and the accuracy of their judgment! The men went on sawing, every now and then pausing in their work to look up at the sky with their backs against the wall. At last there came a moment when the excitement was terrific: the trunk was nearly sawed through, and the tree seemed prepared to fall anywhere and everywhere, more particularly in my direction. Presently it began to give slightly, and it was one of the prettiest and most wonderful things I have ever seen in my life, the way that tree began to bend--gently, gracefully, ever so gently, the trunk fitting itself into the wall, and the branches dashing on to those great boulders that were waiting for them, splitting them up into fragments. Those little mites of Japanese handling that giant of a tree was a sight that I shall never forget. Where we would have had twenty men with ropes and paraphernalia, they had nothing but their big heads and their power to place a thing mathematically in the right position to help them. And it all looked so graceful and so easy that it would not have surprised me in the least to have seen one of those little men come sailing down on the branches. But what struck me the most forcibly was the great confidence of the people. They all stood round, almost touching the tree, but quite sure of the success of this venture; the fact that it was possible for the wood-cutter to fail never occurring to them for an instant.

Placing takes a prominent part in everything that the Japanese undertake; it shows itself not only in the arrangement of the landscape and in artistic matters where there is scope for their decorative powers, but also in small, out-of-the-way, inartistic things, as, for instance, photography. I have seen in the Tokio shop-windows photographs taken by native correspondents during the Chinese war, and it was quite extraordinary how their sense of placing showed itself even in this. You never by any chance see a photograph by a Japanese looking in the least like a European. If they photograph a group of men they will be sure to place that group near a great bough that juts across the picture; they cannot help it--it seems to be in the blood of a Japanese to be decorative. Their taste with regard to enjoyment is widely different from ours: a little bit of Nature which would give them intense pleasure would probably be ignored by us altogether. We want parks and stags and moorlands, broad expanses of country and huge avenues, while the Japanese will be content with one exquisite little harmony. They will gaze for whole hours in rapture at a little branch of peach-blossom, only a cluster, just a few inches of rose-red peach-blossom, with a slim grey twig, placing itself against a background of hills that stretch away in the distance indefinitely.

At the same time they love expanse of view as well. It is one of their greatest joys to look from the top of a mountain downwards, but only at certain times of the day. A Japanese, holiday-making, will sometimes spend one whole day waiting for an effect that will perhaps last only a few moments, or he will toil for hours up a mountain-side to enjoy the exquisite pleasure of a fleeting colour harmony.

ART IN PRACTICAL LIFE

CHAPTER V

ART IN PRACTICAL LIFE

Throughout this book I have talked of Japan purely from the artistic standpoint. I have talked principally of the living art of the country and of its exquisite productions, and I firmly believe that it is because the Japs are a people of imagination that they will at no distant date forge ahead of other nations (who are depending solely upon their muscle) and become a dominating power.

At the same time, it must be clearly understood that the artistic is not the only quality in which the Japs excel. Take them from any side, and it will be found that they have achieved remarkable success. Yet the average Westerner, on returning from a visit to Japan, has always the same superficial observation to make on the Japanese people. He has spent a few weeks in the Land of the Rising Sun; he has seen the dainty tea-houses, the miniature bridges, the paper walls and umbrellas, their works of art modelled in lead--everything suggesting the dainty and the exquisite (and therefore, in his opinion, the flimsy); and he tells you that the people over there are all dear little Noah's Ark folk living in tissue-paper houses, very charming as dolls, but useless as men. "These people," he says, "have no physique; they would be incapable of building battleships, for example." For this critic one can entertain only the faintest possible feeling of tender pity. Is he not aware that these Noah's Ark folk are actually building battleships, that they have already a fine army superbly equipped with the finest of swords and guns, and that they have the power to handle these weapons far better than we can handle ours? Every soldier in the Japanese army understands the mechanism of his rifle, and can at any moment pull it to pieces and put it together again, even substituting a missing portion if necessary. Could the same be said of our beloved Tommy? The Japanese officers are no less capable than the privates, and I would guarantee that if by some mischance the sword of a Japanese officer, being badly tempered, should become bent, that officer would be capable of retempering his blade--one of the most difficult and delicate tasks imaginable.

But how a certain class of equally ignorant and inconsistent Westerners cried out when it was known to the world that Japan had actually begun to use our rifles and to build battleships! They will lose individuality and degenerate, they are adopting Western methods, and it will kill their art, they complained. How foolish this is! The Japanese have merely changed their tools--exchanged the bow and arrow for the sword; they are just as artistic and just as intelligent as in the bow-and-arrow days; and they have proved themselves to be equal to, if not better than, any other soldiers in the world.

Japan is not being Westernised in the smallest degree: she is merely picking our brains. And how quickly the Japs will adopt a Western idea, and improve upon it! The making of matches, and the underselling us in all our common printed cotton and woollen Manchester goods, have not spoilt their faculty for executing that exquisite Eugene dyeing for which the Japanese are famous all the world over; the making of bolts and bars and battleships has not prevented the metal-workers from producing exquisite work in bronze, so delicate as to resemble the finest lace. The manufacture of our vulgar modern monstrosities has been taken up by these people, and they can offer them to us at a cheaper rate and of a better quality than we can produce ourselves, freight included. Japan can produce European work better than the Europeans themselves; but that work has not influenced their art one whit-- they hate it; whereas Japanese art has permeated and influenced the whole of the West.

All these qualities seem to point one way--Japan must eventually become a ruling power. For one thing, the struggle for life does not exist there as in other countries. The food is simple, and men live easily. Then, again, the Japanese are not over-anxious. They do not waste their energies. Women do not fret because they are looking old; on the contrary, it is their ambition to become old, for then they are more respected.

My first experience in Japan, I being a practical person and of a practical turn of mind, was rather a surprise. I had just arrived at the hotel in Tokio, and, observing from my window that there was a promise of a sunset, I caught up my paint-box, anxious to secure the fleeting effect, and rushed downstairs full-tilt, in my haste almost capsizing an old lady with a monkey on her shoulder standing at the foot of the stairs. Not moving from her position, she said, "Young man, I should like to talk to you." "Delighted, I am sure," I answered hurriedly: my haste to be off, I am afraid, was too apparent just then. Not at all daunted, the lady called after me some directions for finding her in her room that night after dinner, where she would tell me some things that would interest me, and walked slowly up the stairs without once looking round, her monkey on her shoulder. Curiously interested, despite myself, in this strange old lady and her monkey, I did visit her that evening, and was somewhat startled by her greeting of me. "I knew I was going to meet you in Japan to-night. I know all about you. You are going to paint a series of pictures. You are going to exhibit them, and you will make a great success.

Some day you will paint children--you are fond of children. All this I knew in America before ever I came here. I saw it all as in a dream." Paralysed, I could only utter the formal words, "Oh, really!" "Ah, you're sceptical! But you are sympathetic too, and after I have talked to you for two or three hours you will see that I am right," quoth my strange new friend, while at the prospect of two or three hours' conversation I experienced a distinctly sinking feeling. But with the next few words she uttered, the sinking feeling vanished, to be superseded by one of deep interest. For some years, she told me, she had been constantly communing in the spirit with her husband and Lord Byron--rival spirits. Her husband was jealous of the poet and of her correspondence with him, and she showed me a series of letters dictated by that great man in the dark--all sorts of beautiful letters on all subjects, ranging from tennis to theology. I sat there I know not how long listening to this wonderful woman; and also--it may seem foolish--I felt strangely comforted and encouraged to hear her say so convincingly that I was to make a success, for at that period I had never painted a picture, and the whole thing was, as it were, an experiment. It was many weeks before I could forget that old lady and her monkey. All through my travels the memory of that monkey's eyes--beady, blinking, never changing--followed me, and stimulated me.

With Tokio and Yokohama I was disappointed. I had the privilege of attending the Mikado's garden party; but the pleasure of the really beautiful grounds and the cherry-blossom was spoilt by the Western dress of the guests and of high personages--a hideous substitute for the Japs' own graceful garments. Yokohama I found especially unsympathetic. The bulk of the Europeans I met there seemed to be spending half their time in abusing Japan and everything Japanese. Strange that a colony of such unrefined, uneducated people should presume to criticise these artists! Tokio, with its formal dinners and conventionalities, was much the same; and with epithets such as "Crank" and "Madman" hurled after me, I fled to Kioto, there to lose myself in endless and undreamt-of joys.

In Japan there are flowers blooming all the year round: the country is a veritable paradise of flowers. When a certain flower is at its height, whether it be the wistaria, the chrysanthemum, or the azalea, that is a signal for a national holiday, and, dropping business and all such minor considerations, the whole of Japan turns out and streams through the parks and through the country to picnic in the sunshine, under the flowers. I arrived in Japan in the spring, and the country was pink with blossom. Infected with the delightful fever for blossom-dreaming, I drifted aimlessly along with the crowds, drifting only too rapidly into their own restful atmosphere, and accustoming myself to the delicious theory that life is long with plenty of time for everything. And as I sat in the sun among these light-hearted people, watching mountains of pink blossom under a clear blue sky, it did seem ridiculous to think of work and worry.

Those first few weeks in Japan come back to me as something to be remembered. To my untravelled mind everything seemed so novel, so quaint, so unexpected. Things were large when I expected them to be small, and vice vers? the houses were made of paper; the women were anxious to make themselves look old. I was fascinated by the pyramids of children gazing in at sweet-stuff shops with their brown, golden, serious faces contrasting so oddly with their gaily-coloured dresses painted to look like butterflies. Every child I saw I felt that I must either pat or give it something. I was surprised to see fowls with tails so long that they had to be wound up into brown-paper parcels; the dogs that mewed like cats; miniature trees hundreds of years old. I was surprised when I dined out to find the room decorated with beautiful ladies in lieu of flowers, a delightful substitute. To be taken to the basement and handed a net with which I was to catch my own carp was also rather a surprise; but when I was expected to eat it as it lay quivering on my plate, I was more than surprised--I was roused. Material for pictures surrounded me at every step. I wanted to make pictures of every pole and signboard that I came across; and the result of this glut of subjects was that I never painted a stroke. Night in Japan fascinated me almost more than anything--the festoons of lanterns crossing from one street to another, yellow-toned with black and vermilion lettering; the gaily-dressed little people passing by on their wooden clogs or in rickshas with swinging paper lanterns drawn by bronze-faced coolies.

I shall never forget my first rainy day in Japan. I went out in the wet and stood there, hatless but perfectly happy, watching the innocent shops light up one by one, and the forest of yellow oil-paper umbrellas with the light shining through looking like circles of gold, ever moving and changing in the purple tones of the street.

One of the first things I did on arriving in Japan was to hire a servant, and this little man soon became my adviser in artistic as well as in mundane matters. He took a keen interest in my work, and spent the greater part of his spare time in hunting up subjects for me--monograms, suggestions for picture-frames, and what not--he, like every Jap, was an artist. He never said that he liked anything that I ever painted (he was far too truthful for that); but it was quite obvious that he did not, for he could draw infinitely better himself. But he helped me a great deal.

So did the policemen--and the policeman in Japan is a perfect treasure. They are all gentlemen of family and are very small men, much below the average in height; but they have nearly all learned the art of scientific wrestling, and exercise an absolute and tyrannical power over the people. Luckily for me, I never made the hopeless blunder of attempting to tip them. Altogether I found the policeman the most delightful person in the world. When I was painting a shop, if a passer-by chanced to look in at a window, he would see at a glance exactly what I wanted; and I would find that that figure would remain there, looking in at the shop, as still as a statue, until I had finished my painting; the policeman meanwhile strutting up and down the street, delighted to be of help to an artist, looking everywhere but at my work, and directing the entire traffic down another street.

Suddenly there is a fire--there is invariably a fire when one arrives in a foreign country, I notice. Immediately the policemen begin to plant little bamboo sticks round the burning building with twine fixed from one stick to another. This is to act as a barrier to keep the people off. After a time a crowd gathers, and in the swaying of the people their chests sometimes touch the string and bow it; but the thought of breaking through that twine never occurs to them. The bold little firemen inside the enclosure trying to scare away the god of fire by bright clothing, and literally sitting on the flames in their light-coloured coats, form a scene never to be forgotten. They seem to bear charmed lives as they dash among the flames, putting the fire out with their hands, and in a very short time too. It reminds one of the performance of the fire-eating gentlemen at the Aquarium.

The power of the policemen over the people in Japan is extraordinary. Even the Westerners obey them. At the treaty ports they often have to deal with English sailors, and, although they try their utmost to smooth things over, they often have to run men in. It is entertaining to see a great blundering sailor, just like a bull, plunging to right and left, while the little policeman, always courteous and polite, constantly gives way, stepping on one side until the time comes when the sailor, puffed and worn out, gives a terrific lunge; the policeman gives him a slight impetus, and the sailor sprawls in an ungainly attitude on the ground. He is then led off triumphantly by a small piece of string attached to his belt behind.

It was not until I arrived in Osaka, the Venice of Japan, that I gave up dreaming and seriously began to work. Here was scope indeed! Osaka is the city of furnaces, factories, and commerce,--the centre of the modern spirit of feverish activity in manufacturing and commercial enterprise. Western ugliness has invaded certain quarters; yet the artistic feeling predominates. The Ajikawa is still the Ajikawa of the olden time, and on the eastern side of the city is the Kizugawa, into which--thanks to the shallowness of the bar--no steamer ever intrudes, while the city itself is intersected by a vast network of canals and waterways, all teeming with junks and barges, and crossed by graceful wooden bridges which lend themselves admirably to line. The Kizugawa fascinates the painter. Away from the bustle of the factories and the shrieking of the whistles, the great junks from northern Hakodate or the sunny Loochos lie sleepily silent. They are the Leviathans of their kind. Intermingling with them are innumerable barges and fishing-boats, stretching far up the river, their masts and cordage seeming one vast spider's web. Not a single vessel is painted--from the huge sea-going junk to the narrow-prowed barge. Near the water-line the wood has taken a silvery tone; but above, it looks in the sunlight like light gold. And the cargoes of rice in straw bales, piled high over the bulwarks, are also golden. A steam-launch has in tow half a dozen barges, which, with their unpainted woodwork, rice bales, and straw-coloured connecting cable, appear against the dark water as a knotted golden thread. In the endless perspective of junks the golden tone predominates; but it is relieved by the colouring of the buildings on the river banks. There is no monotony, for no two houses are similar either in tint or in design; and there is no stiffness of line. The builders are all artists, to whose instincts repetition would do violence. The quaint roofs, although formed in straight lines, seem to rise and fall in gentle undulations. There is nothing abrupt or rugged; nothing jars. And the colours are as varied as the roofs. In the upper reaches of the rivers the scenes never cease to charm. Clusters of half a dozen boats forming a mass of decorative woodwork, tea-houses with tiny gardens running down to the water's edge and gaily-dressed geishas leaning over the trellised verandahs, light bridges thrown in graceful outline against the purple horizon,--all combine to complete a picture as broad as a study by Rembrandt, as infinite in detail as a masterpiece by Hobbema.

THE GARDENS

CHAPTER VI

THE GARDENS

It is not easy to describe the fascination of a Japanese garden. Chiefly it is due to studied neglect of geometrical design. The toy summer-houses dotted here and there, the miniature lakes, and the tiny bridges crossing miniature streams, give an air of indescribable quaintness. Yet, in spite of the smallness of the dimensions, the first impression is one of vastness. "Who discovers that nothingness is law--such a one hath wisdom," says the old Buddhist text. That is the wisdom the Japanese gardener seeks, for he also is an artist. There is no one point on which the eye fastens, and the absence of any striking feature creates a sense of immensity. It is a broad scheme, just as broad as a picture by Velasquez would be, and of infinite detail. It is only accidentally that one discovers the illusion--the triumph of art over space. I saw a dog walk over one of the tiny bridges, and it seemed of enormous height, so that I was staggered at its bulk in proportion to the garden; yet it was but an animal of ordinary size.

A Japanese gardener spends his whole life in studying his trade, and just as earnestly and just as comprehensively as a doctor would study medicine. I was once struck by seeing a little man sitting on a box outside a silk-store on a bald plot of ground. For three consecutive days I saw this little man sitting on the same little box, for ever smiling and knocking out the ash from his miniature pipe. All day long he sat there, never moving, never talking--he seemed to be doing nothing but smoking and dreaming. On the third day I pointed this little man out to the merchant who owned the store, and asked what the little man was doing and why he sat there. "He's thinking," said the merchant. "Yes; but why must he think on that bald plot of ground? What is he going to do?" I asked, perplexed. The merchant gazed at me in astonishment, mingled with pity. "Don't you know," he said, "he is one of our greatest landscape gardeners, and for three days he has been thinking out a garden for me?--If you care to come here in a few days," he added, "I will show you the drawings for that garden all completed." I came in a few days, and I was shown the most exquisite set of drawings it has ever been my good fortune to behold. What a garden it would be! There were full-grown trees, stepping-stones, miniature bridges, ponds of goldfish--all presenting an appearance of vastness, yet in reality occupying an area the size of a small room. And not only was the garden itself planned out and designed, but it was also arranged to form a pattern in relation to the trees and the houses and the surrounding hills. This little old man, without stirring from his box or making a single note, had in those three days created this garden in his mind's eye, and on returning home had sketched out the final arrangement. The merchant told me that his garden would be completed in a few weeks, with full-grown trees flourishing in it, and everything planted--all but one stone, which in all probability would be there in a few weeks, while, on the other hand, it might not be placed there for years. On inquiring as to the reason of this strange delay I was told that that one particular stone, though insignificant and unnoticeable in our eyes, occupies a very prominent position, and that upon the proper placing and quality of it the beauty and perfection of a Japanese garden almost entirely depend. Sometimes hundreds and even thousands of dollars are paid for a large stone that happens to be rightly proportioned and of the correct texture of ruggedness to occupy a certain position in a Japanese garden.

To see the cherry-blossoms of Yoshino, the plum-trees in full bloom at Sugata, the wistaria at Uyeno, or the iris at Horikiri, the people will travel scores of miles. Then, there is the spacious embankment of the Sumidagawa, at the part known as Mukojima, celebrated for its avenue of cherry-trees. Before the Restoration it was the favourite promenade for the daimio and their retainers, and very picturesque it must have been to see the stately nobles in their gorgeous robes, saluting one another with all the grave ceremonial in which the courtiers delighted. The costumes have vanished; but the ancient residences, with their private waterway approaches to the river, remain; and the avenue is still the fashionable promenade.

But it is the iris gardens at Horikiri seen by night that have left an impression which will never fade from my mind. We visited the gardens frequently; but it is one particular visit that I remember above all the others. Leaving the Hotel Metropole late in the afternoon, the ricksha men took us at a rattling pace through the city. After an hour's run we found ourselves far away from the river in the midst of uninviting rice-fields, with a glimpse of the gardens in the distance--a blue and white oasis in a waste of green. If one visits the gardens in the afternoon the changes that the flowers undergo are marvellous. In the full warm rays of the sun, the great petals, turning back towards their stems, are rich and glowing in every shade. Then, as evening comes on and the sunlight fades, the deeper purple blooms lose their richness and grow shadowy, while the white ones take on an icy purity that seems unearthly in its transparency, and they shine as with an internal light. Still a little later, and with the last rays of daylight, all the darker flowers have disappeared, and where a short time ago stood a proud bed of royal colour one can see only the ghastly heads of the pure white petals looming like phantom flowers in the purple night.

The effect of the picture was heightened by the atmospheric colouring. As the silver evening gradually changed to purple night--a purple only seen in Japan--the festoons of lanterns which illuminated the summer-houses became of one colour with the landscape, and then, as the night darkened to a deeper purple, the lights changed to bright orange. It would be impossible to put such colours on canvas: the only way to represent them would be by precious stones. We dined in one of the summer-houses off dainty plates served us by little musm 閣 while seated on the white mats. The blooms of the iris appeared softly luminous, emitting a ghostly light. It is this spiritual beauty which makes the flowers such a favourite in temple gardens, and inspires the Japanese to poetry. On the edge of a tiny lake, approached by a winding walk, through an avenue of bamboo trellis-work, was a small shed with a quaint roof. In the shed the model of a junk was placed. Near it were ink and small strips of paper. The junk was designed to receive poems on the beauty of the iris and of the garden.

Nothing disturbs in a Japanese landscape. It is the harmonic combination of untouched naturalness and high artistic cultivation. The tea-houses owe much of their charm to the absence of paint. The benches, lintels, the posts, are uncoloured, except by age. The white mats and the paper screens act as a foil to the bright flashes of the musm 閣--waiting-girls--who move noiselessly through the rooms like gigantic butterflies flitting to and fro. The iris blooms are a rich mass of colour of blue and white, and the gardener has exhausted his art in pruning all the unnecessary growths without leaving a trace of his handiwork. The ride back was delightful. Tokio at night is seen at its best; the river is then more fascinating. Huge junks, with a solitary light at the masthead, glide by--fantastic shadows in the purple haze. The tea-houses, with their festoons of lanterns and orange interiors, in which one caught glimpses of singing girls in their brilliant dresses, gleamed like golden patches in the cool purple. The bridges sparkled with lights; the shops were bright with colour; and all through the city, to enjoy the coolness of the night air, groups of citizens were seated in the streets chattering as gaily and as light-heartedly as only the Japs can.

FLOWER ARRANGEMENT

CHAPTER VII

FLOWER ARRANGEMENT

One of the chief characteristics of the Japanese, which especially distinguishes them from Europeans, is their intense fondness for flowers--not the fondness which many English people affect, but an instinctive love of the beautiful, and a poetical appreciation of symbolism. The Japanese nature is artistic in essence, and in no more delightful manner is the art of the people expressed than in the cultivation of flowers. Flowers to them are a source of infinite and unending joy, of which the chief pleasure lies in their proper placing and arrangement. Every common Japanese workman, every fan-worker or metal-worker, has some little flower carefully placed beside him at his work; he loves and prunes and cares for it.

If you dine out with a friend you will be seated, not on the right-hand side of the past-middle-age lady of the house, but near some beautiful flower. The "honoured interior" would never have the presumption to seat you next herself. You are her guest, and must be made happy by being placed in the near neighbourhood of the principal and most beautiful object in the room, which is invariably the arrangement of flowers. And a vase of flowers in a Japanese house is at once a picture and a poem, being always in perfect harmony with the surroundings. The art of arranging flowers is an exact science, in the study of which seven years of constant hard work finds a man but fairly proficient. In fact, to create a really fine arrangement is just as difficult as to paint an equally fine picture. Every leaf and every flower has to be drawn and practically modelled into form, whlle even so simple a thing as the bending of a twig requires much care and knowledge. To become a master in the art of flower-arrangement a man must study for at least fourteen years, devoting the remainder of his life to perfecting and improving it.

There are scores of different arrangements that one must learn, and volumes upon volumes of designs, showing all the most delicate and subtle forms of placing which a master, in order to create perfect balance, must have at his fingers' ends. These ancient designs are so perfect that it is almost impossible to change them or to insert any original work into them. Here and there, indeed, some great master will make a slight variation in the arrangement of a particular flower, and in a very short time that variation is trumpeted throughout the country and known in all art sections. To a Westerner this seems incredible. He affirms that if he jumbles a bunch of flowers together in a vase he can create a different effect every time. Very probably, and he can also strew roses and cut flowers all over his dining-table if he likes; but he will still be creating nothing more than a jumble. If he were to think out the arrangement of his table from an artistic point of view as a bit of decoration, he would find it impossible to produce such a wealth of inartistic variety. "But," argues the uninitiated Westerner, "these roses strewn carelessly over our tables, and bunches of flowers stuck loosely into vases, are far more natural than the single stiff bough of blossom of Japanese decoration. Flowers grow in Nature carelessly and wildly, and therefore they must be arranged to look like that." Now, it is always difficult to answer these people, for the dining-table of the West begins by being utterly hopeless in decoration and in colour. One cannot possibly compare this meaningless attire, this independent mass of colour forming no pattern, and probably placed upon the table by a servant without care or thought, and with an utter disregard to form and order,--one cannot compare such decoration with the beautiful, scientifically-thought-out flower arrangements of Japan. All that one can say is that one is art and the other is not. Nature grabbed at in this crude Western fashion and stuck into a vase is no longer Nature.

Consummate naturalness is brought about only by consummate art, and is not the result of accident. If a bough of blossom growing in the midst of other trees is taken from Nature and placed in a vase, however beautiful it might originally have been, it must necessarily appear awkward and out of place. One of the chief characteristics of Japanese flower arrangement is its resemblance to the flowers in a state of nature. A bough or a tree in a Japanese room looks exactly like a real bit of Nature lifted bodily out of the sunshine and its own particular surroundings, and placed there. Nature appears to be almost commonplace as compared with the work of a great Japanese master in the art of flower arrangement, and almost less natural. A master, after having received a clear impression of the way a certain bough appears in the midst of its background of Nature, is capable of taking that single bough and of twisting it into broad beautiful lines, one picking up with the other in such a way as to convey the same impression to you as it did when growing in its own sunny garden.

"But why are there so few flowers in this Japanese method of flower decoration?" complains the Westerner. "Why only one branch of blossom in a pot?--why only one?" Because you can see that one and enjoy it, provided that you have the capacity to see at all, which the majority of people have not. One beautiful bough or one beautiful picture should be ample food for enjoyment to last an artist for one whole day. If there were twenty beautiful boughs, or twenty beautiful pictures, you would look from one to the other and would necessarily become confused. You would leave that room feeling thoroughly unhappy, and with the same sort of headache that one gets after spending an afternoon in a picture-gallery. To enjoy one of these pictures or flowers, and to concentrate one's thoughts upon it alone, you would have to frame it between your hands, cutting it off and isolating it from the rest.

This the Japanese do for you. They know that you cannot appreciate more than one beautiful object at a time, and they see that that one object is perfectly placed in relation to its surroundings, so as to give rest and enjoyment to the eye. Almost every one in Japan, either young or old, is capable of appreciating a fine arrangement of flowers, and nearly every Japanese woman can practise the art.

So many minute descriptions have already been written of the methods of the masters of flower decoration that there is little else to say on that point. However, since decoration by flowers has so much to do with the art of the country, and is so closely connected with the character of the people, I feel that I must give a slight description of some of the marvellous creations in purple irises, lilies, and pines that the greatest master in Tokio once arranged for me at my hotel. He arrived early one morning, and in great good-humour, evidently feeling that, I being an artist, his work would be appreciated and understood. He carried with him his flowers, tenderly wrapped in a damp cloth under one arm, and his vases under another. One of his most promising pupils, a girl of nineteen, accompanied him, acting almost as a servant and evidently worshipping him as her master. He began at once to show us a decoration of lilies and reeds. With the utmost rapidity he took out a bunch of slim reeds, pulled them to different lengths, the large ones at the back, the small ones in front, and caressed the whole into a wooden prong looking like a clothes-peg, and arranged it in a kind of vase made out of a circular section of bamboo. An immense amount of care was taken with the handling of these reeds, the master drawing back now and then in a stooping position with his hands on his knees and his eyes bolting out to view his handiwork critically. Next he took some lilies with their leaves, and arranged them in a metal stand composed of a number of divisions looking like cartridge-cases cut off. Every leaf was twisted and bent and cut to improve its form. The half-open lilies were made to look as though they were growing, and were a great favourite with this master because of the scope for beautiful curves and lines that they allowed. Time after time he would take out a leaf or a flower, putting another in its place, thereby showing that he had absolute command over his subject, and a fixed picture in his mind that he was determined to produce at any cost. The ultimate result of the decoration was perfect naturalness. I never saw lilies growing on the hillside look more natural than they did here; yet each had been twisted and bent into a set design laid down by the artist. Both reeds and lilies were placed in a wooden tray partially lacquered, the unlacquered portion representing old worm-eaten wood; pebbles were placed in the bottom of the tray, and the whole was flooded with water. Then he began his decoration of irises. He took a bundle of iris leaves, cut and trimmed them, washing and drying each leaf separately, and sticking them together in groups of twos and threes. With his finger and thumb he gently pressed each one down the centre, rendering it as pliable as wire. The leaves were cut to a point at the base and placed in a metal stand with consecutive circles. Then an iris bud, with the purple just bursting, was placed in position and caressed into bloom. The whole was syringed with water and carefully placed in a corner of the room.

I have described these few flower arrangements in detail in order to show the exactitude of the work and the immense amount of care taken by professors in flower arrangement. On this particular occasion I had invited some friends to enjoy the professor's masterpieces with me, and he had just completed a most exquisite production, by far the best and finest he had achieved that day. It was an arrangement of pine with one great jutting bough, perfectly balanced--in fact, a veritable work of art. The professor was a true artist; he loved his work, and it was all the world to him.

For once he was content, and had just leant back to view his work through half-closed eyes when in a flash an Oxford straw hat was clapped down right on top of it. It was the husband of one of my friends just returned from a walk, full of spirits and boisterously happy. It was a cruel thing to do; but he did not realise the horror of his act. He saw a bough sticking right out of a pot, and it seemed to him a suitable place to hang his hat on: so he hung it there--that was all. The little assistant gave one frightened look at her master, and began to pack up the utensils at once; the professor drew himself up in a very dignified way, bowed profoundly, and left the hotel. I never saw him again, and I knew that I never should--for he went away crushed.

THE GEISHA

CHAPTER VIII

THF GEISHA

With all their practical gifts--which, as one of themselves has remarked, will enable them to beat the world with the tips of their fingers--and all the power of assimilating and adapting to their own purposes the best that other nations have to offer them,--the Japanese are essentially and beyond all a nation of artists. It is not only in the work-shop and the studio, but also in the simplest act and detail of daily life, that this sense of the decorative oozes unconsciously forth, and most of all, and most unconsciously, in the Japanese woman--the geisha.

The raison d'tete of the geisha is to be decorative. She delights in her own delightsomeness; she wants frankly to be as charming as nature and art will allow; she wants to be beautiful; and she honestly and assuredly wants me and you and the stranger artists to think her beautiful. She wants to please you, and she openly sets about pleasing, taking you into her confidence (so to speak) as to her methods. She does it with the simple joy and sincerity of a child dressing up. There is no mock shyness, no fan put up, no screen drawn, no pathetic struggle to deceive you into belief in the reality of an all-too-artificial peach-bloom; there is nothing of the British scheme--no powder-puff hidden in a pocket-handkerchief, no little ivory box with a looking-glass in the lid, no rouge-tablet concealed in a muff to be supplied surreptitiously at some propitious moment. The Japanese woman has the courage to look upon her face purely as so much surface for decoration, a canvas upon which to paint a picture; and she decorates it as one might decorate a bit of bare wall. The white is simple vegetable white; the red is pure vermilion toning with her kimono. The white makes no effort to blend with the natural tone of her neck: it announces itself in a clear-cut, knife-edge pattern above the folds of the kimono.

I remember a little story that I once heard (it was told me by the designer of the waterworks in Tokio)--only a trifling incident; but it struck me as being thoroughly typical of the na 阃 e, almost childish simplicity of the Japanese woman. It was on the day that the waterworks were completed, and the high officials and their wives were being escorted over the works in trucks, in order that they might see and admire this great engineering feat, of which my friend, the architect, was very justly proud. There were two trucks--one for the men and one for their wives. The truck containing the men was wheeled up under a shaft where the light came down from above, and enabled the officials to look up and admire this great work. The men looked up and were duly impressed, and altogether the experiment passed off successfully. Then the idea was that they should move aside so as to allow the women also to enjoy the spectacle. No sooner was the truck-load of women drawn up beneath the shaft than their faces lit up with pleased surprise, and every woman whipped out a looking-glass and a rouge-pot and began to decorate her face. Not one of them looked up, or even attempted to take the slightest notice of the waterworks: all they knew was that it afforded them just sufficient light by which to decorate themselves, and they promptly made use of it.

The geisha is the educated woman of Japan. She is the entertainer, the hostess; she is highly educated, and has a great appreciation of art; she is also proficient in the art of conversation. The geisha begins her career at a very early age. When only two or three years old she is taught to sing and dance and talk, and above all to be able to listen sympathetically, which is the greatest art of all. The career of this tiny mite is carved out thus early because her mother foresees that she has the qualities that will develop, and the little butterfly child, so gay and so brilliant, will become a still more gorgeous butterfly woman. Nothing can be too brilliant for the geisha; she is the life and soul of Japan, the merry sparkling side of Japanese life; she must be always gay, always laughing and always young, even to the end of her life. But for the girl who is to become the ordinary domesticated wife it is different. Starting life as a bright, light-hearted little child, she becomes sadder and sadder in colour and in spirits with every passing year. Directly she becomes a wife her one ambition is to become old--in fact, it is almost a craze with her. She shows it in every possible way--in the way she ties her obi, the fashion in which she dresses her hair; everything that suggests the advance of the sere and yellow leaf she will eagerly adopt. When her husband gives a party he calls in the geisha; she herself, poor dear, sits upstairs on a mat and is not allowed to be seen. She is called the "honoured interior," and is far too precious and refined to figure in public life. But, mind you, this little married lady, the "honoured interior," does not ignore her personal appearance altogether: she too will never miss an opportunity to whip out the rouge-pot and mirror that always form part of every Japanese woman's attire in order to decorate her face. And although to our eyes she appears a nonentity as compared with the geisha, her position is in reality a very happy one and greatly to be envied. What if the geisha entertain her husband's guests? Hers is the greater privilege of attending upon him when he returns, tired out from the festivities; she is as a rare jewel set in the background of her home, and the "honoured interior" is perfectly content.

But the idiotic idea so general in the West, that the geisha is a silly giggling little girl with a fan, must really be corrected, although I can quite understand how this opinion has been formed. The geisha in reality is a little genius, perfectly brilliant as a talker, and mistress of the art of dancing. But she knows that the Westerner does not appreciate or understand her fine classical dancing and singing, and she is so refined and so charming that she will not allow you to feel that you are ignorant and more or less vulgar, but will instantly begin to amuse you in some way that she thinks you will enjoy and understand. She will perhaps unfold paper and draw rapid character-sketches of birds and fish, or dance a sort of spirited dance that she feels will entertain you. It is very seldom that they will show you their fine classical dances; but if by good fortune you can over-persuade them, as I have done, the sight is one that you will never forget--the slow, dignified movements, the placing of the foot and the hand, the exquisite curves and poses of the body, forming a different picture every time,--all is a joy and a perfect intellectual treat to the artist and to the lover of beautiful things. There is no rushing about, no accordion skirt and high kick, nothing that in any way resembles the Western dance.

Sometimes, if she finds that you appreciate the fine work, the geisha will give you imitations of the dancing on our stage at home, and although it is very funny, the coarseness of it strikes you forcibly. One never dines out or is entertained in Japan without the geisha forming a prominent part of the entertainment; in fact, she herself decorates the room where you are dining, just as a flower or a picture would decorate our dining-rooms at home, only better. And there is nothing more typical of the decorative sense innate in the Japanese than the little garden of geisha girls, which almost invariably forms the background of every tea-house dinner. The dinner itself, with its pretty doll-tables, its curious assortment of dainty viands set in red lacquer bowls, its quaint formalities, and the magnificent ceremonial costumes of its hosts, is an artistic scheme, elaborately thought out and prepared. But when, at the close, the troupe of geishas and ma 颽 os appears, forming (as it were) a pattern of gorgeous tropical flowers, the scene becomes a bit of decoration as daring, original, and whimsically beautiful as any to be seen in the land of natural "placing" and artistic design and effect. The colours of kimonos, obis, fans, and head-ornaments blend, contrast, and produce a carefully-arranged harmony, the whole converging to a centre of attraction, a grotesque, fascinating, exotic figure, the geisha of geishas--that vermilion-and-gold girl who especially seizes me. She is a bewildering symphony in vermilion, orange, and gold. Her kimono is vermilion embroidered in great dragons; her obi is cloth of gold; her long hanging sleeves are lined with orange. Just one little slim slip of apple-green appears above the golden fold of the obi and accentuates the harmony; it is the crape cord of the knapsack which bulges the loops at the back and gives the Japanese curve of grace. The little apple-green cord keeps the obi in its place, and is the discord which makes the melody.

My vermilion girl's hair is brilliant black with blue lights, and shining where it is stiffened and gummed in loops and bands till they seem to reflect the gold lacquer and coral-tipped pins that bristle round her head. Yes, she is like some wonderful fantastical tropical blossom, that vermilion geisha-girl, or like some hitherto unknown and gorgeous dragon-fly. And she is charming; so sweetly, simply, candidly alluring. Every movement and gesture, each rippling laugh, each fan-flutter, each wave of her rice-powdered arms from out of their wing-like sleeves, is a joyous and naive appeal for admiration and sympathy. How impossible to withhold either! The geisha-girl is an artist: I am an artist: we understand each other.

My geisha-girl brings out her dainty lacquer-box, and under the gaze of all sits down to decorate herself with a frank joy in the pleasure she knows she is going to give. And she knows too what she is about. She knows the value of a tone in a lip. Something suggests to her that you, an artist, may have found the vermilion lip not quite in harmony with the plan, and she changes it to bronze. Three times this evening does my geisha-girl change her lip; she frankly takes it off with a little bit of rice-paper, which she rolls up and tucks into the folds of her kimono, to be thrown away later, and the bronze lip is substituted. By and by it seems to occur to her that the bronze lip has become monotonous, and she will change it again to vermilion. No doubt before the evening is over there will be a series of little bits of rice-paper folded away ready to be got rid of when the bill is paid, the supper eaten, and the festival at an end.

It is through the geisha-girls that there is still a living art in Japan at the present day in the designs of the silk dresses that they wear. They are so modern, so up-to-date, and yet so characteristic of Japan. The women are very extravagant in their dress, and some of the leading geisha-girls will often go to the length of having stencils, with elaborate designs and an immense amount of hand-work, specially cut for them, the stencils and designs being destroyed when sufficient material for one dress has been supplied. For such a unique and costly gown the geisha will of course have to pay a fabulous sum, and a sum that would astound the average English woman of fashion. But then when a geisha orders a costume she thinks it out carefully; she does not go, as we do, to a dressmaker, but to an artist. It may be that she has a fancy for apple-blossom at sunset, and this idea she talks out with the artist who is to draw the designs.

A Japanese woman chooses her costumes, not according to fashion but to some sentiment or other--apple-blossom because it is spring-time, peach-blossom for a later season,--and many beautiful ideas are thus expressed in the gowns of the women of Japan. But although the geisha has plenty of latitude in which to display her artistic feeling, there are some little details of etiquette and fashion that she must adhere to, which show themselves in a few details of the Japanese women's attire, as, for example, in the thongs of her little wooden shoes and the decoration of her jet-black hair. Not only is the kimono of the geisha, its colour and design, thought out by the artist, but all the accessories of her toilette, such as the obi, the fan, and the ornaments for her hair. It is the artist's ambition that she should be a picture, perfect in every detail, and the geisha is always a picture, beautiful beyond description.

How different she is from the geisha of fiction, of operettas, and of story-books, which is the only geisha that the stay-at-home Englishman can know! That she is beautiful to look at all the world agrees; but quite apart from her beauty, or the social position that she happens to occupy in Japan, take her as a woman, a real woman, stripped of all outward appearances and of her own particular nationality--take her as a woman, and she will be found as dainty in mind as in appearance, highly educated, and with a great sense of honour, while her moral code would compare favourably with others of her sex all the world over.

CHILDREN

CHAPTER IX

CHILDREN

A cluster of little Japanese children at play somehow suggests to me a grand picture-gallery, a picture-gallery of a nation. Every picture is a child upon which has been expended the subtle decorative sense of its family or neighbours, as expressed in the tint of its dress and sash and in the decoration of its little head. It is in the children that the national artistic and poetic nature of the Japanese people most assuredly finds expression. Each little one expresses in its tiny dress some conception, some idea or thought, dear to the mother, some particular aspect of the national ideals. And just as in the West the character of a man can be gauged by the set and crease of his trousers, so in Japan are the sentiments and ideals of a mother expressed in the design and colouring of her baby's little kimono. Thus, when watching a group of children, maybe on a fête day, one instinctively compares them with a gallery of pictures, each of which is a masterpiece, painted by an artist whose individuality is clearly expressed therein. Each little picture in this gallery of children is perfect in itself; yet on closer study it will be found that the children are more than mere pictures. They tell us of the truths of Japan.

One child, in the clearness and freshness of its dress, seems to embody an expression of that unselfish cheerfulness so characteristic of the Japanese, among whose children you can go for days without seeing one cry. Another, in the graceful dignity and rich yet severe colouring of its costume, tells of that faithful spirit of loyalty and pride that has always marked the lives of the Japanese. One tiny baby, in the dainty sombreness of colour and quiet arrangement of the folds of its little kimono, suggests the thoughtful consideration and sweet seriousness of the women of Japan; and another child, dressed in a wonderful combination of red and bronze relieved by glimpses of white, expresses in its rich glowing colour, and the purity of the white within, the fire of Japanese patriotism.

But come with me for a walk on any day, in sun or in rain, whether on a gala day or on an ordinary day, and we shall meet little units in the decorative whole, every one of them a colour picture bringing to the mind some characteristic of the people. We shall find one little one who, to the eye of the artist, flashes like a gem, her white kimono, decorated, or rather made vivid, as by the hand of a master, with only three or four great black crosses, each formed of the crisp dexterous drags across the surface of the cloth. Again the black is repeated in the carefully-arranged hair, and the white in the little wooden shoes; but all is toned and touched by just a little old rose in the ribbon that ties her head-dress and the fastening of the thongs at her feet.

Such an art in a people is living; it has its root in national spirit and national character, and must continue to foster and strengthen the national ideals.

The clothing of her children is a matter of great and serious consideration to the Japanese mother. When a baby is born she gathers together all her friends, and they discuss a scheme of decoration for the set of miniature dresses that the little one is to wear. More care is taken with these baby dresses than with those of any grown person, and if the parents are rich the sums that are spent on silk crepe are sometimes such as would shock any English mother. So much has to be taken into consideration with regard to the design of a child's dress: it might be cherry-blossom or a landscape, according to the month and the circumstances amid which the infant was born. The colouring of the costume is generally suggestive of the ideas and sentiments of the mother. She does not say, "I will take this bough of apple-blossom, and it shall be the dress of my child," or "I will take Fuji at sunset, and the colouring of my baby's dress shall be of old rose and white snow." She does not grab at nature in this crude way; but the artistic and poetical feelings innate in her unconsciously find expression in the little frock. When the mother and her neighbours have finally decided upon a scheme of decoration, the designs are placed in the hands of some great artist, who carries them out in water-colour drawings on silk, which the friends gather together again to examine and generally enjoy. Then the designs are handed over to some expert stencil-cutter, go through the regular elaborate course, and are finally retouched, by the artist himself, directly on to the silk. If the parents are rich enough the stencils are destroyed, and the dress consequently becomes unique. Such a dress will doubtless be an exquisite work of art, and very costly. Indeed, a dress for a Japanese baby can cost quite as much as a picture by a leading Academician, and is of far greater artistic value. But no price can be too great, no colouring too gorgeous, for the dresses of these little butterflies, the children of Japan. The poorest mother will scrape together sufficient money, and the father sacrifice one half of his daily portion of rice, in order that a child may attend a festival in the bright hues befitting its age. The younger the child, the more brilliant is its dress. You will see a mite, a little baby girl that cannot walk or talk, clothed in silk crepe of the most brilliant colour possible--rainbow colour, almost prismatic in its brilliancy. As the child grows older the colours fade, and become duller, until by the time she is a full-grown woman they have sobered down almost to Quaker hues--except here and there, where some tiny edging of colour shows itself.

The science of deportment occupies quite half the time of the Japanese children's lives, and so early are they trained that even the baby of three, strapped to the back of its sister aged five, will in that awkward position bow to you and behave with perfect propriety and grace. This Japanese baby has already gone through a course of severe training in the science of deportment. It has been taught how to walk, how to kneel down, and how to get up again without disarranging a single fold of its kimono. After this it is necessary that it should learn the correct way to wait upon people--how to carry a tray, and how to present it gracefully; while the dainty handing of a cup to a guest is of the greatest importance imaginable. A gentleman can always tell the character of a girl and the class to which she belongs by the way she offers him a cup of Sake. And then the children are taught that they must always control their feelings--if they are sad, never to cry; if they are happy, to laugh quietly, never in a boisterous manner, for that would be considered vulgar in the extreme.

Modesty and reserve are insisted upon in the youth of Japan. A girl is taught that she must talk very little, but listen sympathetically to the conversation of her superiors. If she has a brother, she must look up to him as her master, even although he be younger than herself. She must give way to him in every detail. The baby boy places his tiny foot upon his sister's neck, and she is thenceforth his slave. If he is sad, her one care must be to make him happy. Her ambition is to imitate as nearly as possible the behaviour of her mother towards her own lord and master.

Many attempts have been made by enterprising Westerners to "broaden" the minds of the Japanese girls, and to make them more independent, by establishing schools for them, where they can be educated on purely Western principles; but these attempts have always failed. The women turned out from such establishments are always unhappy, and continue to suffer for the rest of their lives, because they are disliked and resented by all their people, and no man will marry any of them. The beautiful side of life seems to have been taken from them; imagination is crushed and spoilt; they are unfitted for the life that every Japanese woman must lead. Naturally they are hated by the men, for the womanly qualities that are most valuable in a Japanese girl are destroyed by this Western "broadening" of their minds: they wear high-heeled shoes, put nosegays on the table, and are altogether demoralised. Sad to say, Western influence is keenly felt within the schools which belong to all classes and conditions of Japanese children, and one trembles lest gradually the simplicity and quaint formality of their bringing-up should become hardened and roughened into the system which has done so much to spoil the child-life of the West. Their own artistic training is perfect; and although Japan is the land of ceremony, and the children are brought up with a certain strictness of propriety unknown in the less ceremonious West, their utter naturalness and absolute freedom from seeking after effects present in them a simplicity of character which helps to make them the most delightful of their kind. A little boy flying a kite is like no other boy you have ever seen in England. There is a curious formality and staidness about him and his companions which never degenerates into shyness.

Once I drifted into a country village in search of subjects for pictures, and I found to my astonishment that every living soul there was flying a kite, from old men down to babies. It was evidently a f陰e day, dedicated to kites; all business seemed abandoned, and every one either stood or ran about, gazing up in the air at the respective toys. There were kites of every variety--red kites, yellow kites, kites in the shape of fish, teams of fighting kites, and sometimes whole battalions of them at war with kites of a different colour, attempting to chafe each other's strings. It rather surprised me at first to see staid old men keenly interested in so childish an amusement; but in a very short time I too found myself running about with the rest, grasping a string and watching with the greatest joy imaginable the career of a floating thing gorgeously painted, softly rising higher and higher in the air, until it mingled among the canopy of other kites above my head, becoming entangled for a moment, then leaving them and soaring up above the common herd, and side by side with a monstrous butterfly kite; then came the chase, the fight, and the downfall of one or the other. They were all children there, every one of them, from the old men downwards; all care and worry was for the time forgotten in the simple joy of flying kites; and I too, in sympathy with the gaiety about me, felt bubbling over with pure joy. To see these lovely flower-like child faces mingling with the yellow wrinkled visages of very old men, all equally happy in a game in which age played no part, was an experience never to be forgotten. None was too old or too young, and you would see mites strapped to the backs of their mothers, holding a bit of soiled knotted string in their baby fingers, and gazing with their black slit eyes at some tiny bit of a crumpled kite floating only a few inches away.

Another game in which both the youth and the age of Japan play equal parts is the game of painting sand-pictures on the roadside. These sand-pictures are often executed by very clever artists; but I have seen little children drawing exquisite pictures in coloured sands. Japanese children seem to have an instinctive knowledge of drawing and a facility in the handling of a paint-brush that is simply extraordinary. They will begin quite as babies to practise the art of painting and drawing, and more especially the art of painting sand-pictures. You will see groups of little children sitting in the playground of some ancient temple, each child with three bags of coloured sand and one of white, competing with one another as to who shall draw the quaintest and most rapid picture. The white sand they will first proceed to spread upon the ground in the form of a square, cleaning the edges until it resembles a sheet of white paper. Then, with a handful of black sand held in the chubby fingers, they will draw with the utmost rapidity the outline of some grotesque figure of a man or an animal, formed out of their own baby imaginations. Then come the coloured sands, filling in the spaces with red, yellow, or blue, according to the taste and fancy of the particular child artist. But the most extraordinary and most fascinating thing of all is to watch the performance of a master in sand-pictures. So dexterous and masterly is he that he will dip his hand first into a bag of blue sand, and then into one of yellow, allowing the separate streams to trickle out unmixed; and then with a slight tremble of the hand these streams will be quickly converted into one thin stream of bright green, relapsing again into the streams of blue and yellow at a moment's notice. A Japanese mother will take infinite pains to cultivate the artistic propensities of her child, and almost the first lesson she teaches it is to appreciate the beauties of nature. She will never miss the opportunity of teaching the infant to enjoy the cherry-blossom on a sunny day in Uyeno Park. Hundreds of such little parties are to be seen under the trees enjoying the blossom, while the mother, seated in the middle of the group, points out the many beauties of the scene. She will tell them dainty fairy stories--to the boys, brave deeds of valour, to strengthen their courage; to the girls, tales of unselfish and honourable wives and mothers. Every story has a moral attached to it, and is intended to educate and improve the children in one direction or another. There is one fairy story which is a universal favourite with both mothers and children, and that is the story of Momotaro. When seeing a mother talking earnestly to her children, I have always discovered that it was the same old story, old yet ever fresh. It is a curiously simple tale about an old woman who goes every day to the river to wash clothes, and an old man who goes to the mountain to fetch wood. The old woman is always unhappy because she has no children, and one day, when she is washing clothes in the river, a large peach comes floating down towards her. On carrying it home, she hears the cry of a child, which appears to come from the inside of the peach. She rapidly cuts it in two, and finds to her amazement a fine baby sitting in the middle of it, which, since it was born in a peach, she afterwards called Momotaro. The story then goes on to tell how the baby grows up to be a fine healthy lad, who, on reaching the age of seventeen, plans an expedition to subjugate an island of the devil. A minute description is given of the food he takes with him--of the corn and rice wrapped in a bamboo leaf--and how on his journey he meets with a wasp, a crab, a chestnut, and a millstone, who all promise to help him if he will give them half of his food. The lad complies, and a beautiful description is given of their journey to the island of the devil, on which journey a very skilful plan is thought out by which to kill him. On arriving at the island, they find that the chief of the devils is not in his own room. They soon take advantage of his absence. The chestnut hops into the ash; the millstone mounts on to the roof; the crab hides in the washing-pan; the wasp settles in a corner; and the lad waits outside. The poor devil comes back, and has a terrible time between them all. He goes to the fireplace to warm his hands; the chestnut cracks in the fire and burns them; he rushes to the water-pan to cool himself, and the crab bites his hand; he flies to a safe place, and is tormented by the wasp; in an agony of pain he tries to leave the room, but the remorseless millstone descends with a crash upon his head, and mortally wounds him. This story is told to the Japanese children over and over again, but is always received with wide-eyed delight and excitement.

I have never seen a child in Japan cry; nor have I ever seen one smacked, for what mother can have the heart to touch so dainty a blossom as the child flower of this land of flowers? A group of Japanese children is perhaps the prettiest sight on earth, and they themselves are works of art, the beauty of which can scarcely be imagined. Each head and each piquant face is but a field where the ever-present artist can exercise his ingenuity and his skill in colour and design. Deliberately the child's head and face are treated as subjects fit for the most decorative of design, and the result, though quaint and formal to the last degree, is invariably as pleasing as it is undoubtedly startling and original. And the children themselves are no less full of interest than their heads and faces are full of paint. I once saw a pyramid of children gazing in at a sweet-stuff shop. They looked like three children; but on closer inspection I discovered that one was a doll looking about the age of a child of two, with its great head lolling on the back of its mother, aged three. The three-year-old was a boy, strapped to the back of his sister aged five. The doll and the sister looked very sleepy and tired as they gazed vacantly at the rows of tempting pink sugar-water bottles in the sweet-stuff shop; but what arrested my attention was the alert and intelligent expression of the three-year-old child in the middle, who, just as I took out my notebook to sketch the group, put a lighted cigarette between his lips, holding it between two chubby fingers, eyeing me with the peculiar introspective look of the old hand as he both tests the excellence of the tobacco and gives himself up to its enjoyment. As I sketched him he looked composedly at me out of his big eyes, and posed twice without a particle of artificiality--once with the cigarette in his mouth, and again as if he had just taken it from his lips for a moment while he paid attention to me.

I remember once passing a temple, an ancient Shinto temple called "Kamogamo"; it was a sacred temple and very popular, being much frequented for picnics. On this particular day there was going on one of the two important picnics or festivals of the year; the great ground of the temple and the playground were enclosed about with straw ropes on bamboo poles, to separate one from another. It was a festival for girls under ten, and there were hundreds of children, all with their kimonos tucked up, showing their scarlet petticoats, and looking for all the world like a mass of poppies. The scarlet in the petticoats was universally repeated in neck and hair; but their kimonos varied much, and were of almost every shade and texture of Japanese cloth and silk crepe imaginable. There were luminous greens, fawns, stripes, golden browns shading into lemon-yellows, harmonies in brown and violet, and dresses striped and chequered in tones of almost every conceivable value. Two rows or armies of these girls were placed several yards distant from each other in this long emerald-green field; and in the space between them stood two servants, each holding a long bamboo pole, fresh and green, being evidently just cut down for the fair, and suspending from its top a flat shallow drum covered with tissue paper. Presently two young men teachers appeared on the scene carrying two baskets of small many-coloured balls, which they threw down on the grass between the children and the drums. Then a signal was given, and all the girls started running down the field at full tilt towards one another, pouncing on the balls as they ran, and throwing them with all their force up at the paper drums. The great majority of them missed their aim altogether, and flew either above or below the drums, some of the mites getting so excited that they threw the balls forty or fifty yards in mid air. After a time, when a perfect shower of balls had passed through the tissue drums, quite demolishing them, a shower of coloured papers, miniature lanterns, paper umbrellas, and flags came slowly fluttering down among the children on to their jet-black bobbing heads, and into their eager outstretched hands. Never have I seen anything more beautiful than these gay, brightly-clad people, packed closely together like a cluster of flowers in the brilliant sparkling sunshine, with their pretty upturned faces watching the softly falling rain of coloured toys. I strolled through the temple grounds, passed this brilliant stream of colour and lovely laughing children, passed the cherry-trees and dainty tea-houses, and in a few minutes found myself in a cool grey-green forest of bamboo, an academic bamboo grove looking like a pillared temple, sunless and silent. It was here that the philosophers of old taught and meditated, and it seemed a place to meditate in--so quiet, so sombre, shut off from the world with its endless lofty pillars of grey luminous green--silent, a world apart.

WORKERS

CHAPTER X

WORKERS

It was with a view to decorating my newly-built London house that I paid a second visit to Japan, being convinced that it was possible to handle the labour there at a cheaper rate and with finer results than in Europe. My experience proved that I was right. Before leaving England, however, I was carefully informed by all my friends of the exceedingly bad reputation that the Japanese have gained commercially. I was told that they were treacherous and unscrupulous in their dealings, and that I was, above all, to beware of the Japanese merchant. As it happened, it was through making a friend of one particular little Japanese merchant--through concentrating my attention upon him, and studying him continually--that I was enabled to gain a real insight into the life of the people, and to tear away that impenetrable veil which, to the Westerner's eyes, always hangs before them.

When you get to know a Japanese merchant well, a man who has studied our methods, you will find that he talks openly and frankly about his dealings with the European globe-trotter. He will tell you that he cheats you and charges you high prices because the average Westerner has got no eye. The Westerner does not appreciate the really fine and beautiful articles that the Japanese soul worships; therefore the merchant gives him what he thinks the Westerner wants, and asks the price that he thinks the traveller will give. When we first came into touch with the Japanese we began by cheating them and foisting deceptions upon them, and now they simply turn the tables upon us and cheat us to the best of their ability. The only difference is that the Japanese have more intelligence about wrong done them, and their motive for cheating is thus resentingly greater. I have had many dealings with the Japanese myself, and have always found them just. To be sure, I have never come into touch with the treaty-port merchants, who have been more or less tainted by the Westerner; but I have come into touch with, and studied, the genuine workers of Japan.

My first object on arriving in Tokio was to find some Japanese who would be capable of gathering together a series of splendid craftsmen to work for me. As luck would have it, I found my man--a perfect little genius of a fellow--on the evening of my first day in Japan, and in a most unexpected manner. I was sitting in the reading-room of the hotel, with my plans spread out before me, dreaming of the Japanese glories that were to decorate my London house, when my attention was attracted by seeing a little creature, looking like a monkey with a great box on his back, bound suddenly into the room, evidently by aid of the manager's foot in the adjoining hall. Not in the least perturbed, he began to unstrap the box from his back, from which he took out curios, and drifted about the room trying to sell them to the different globe-trotters assembled there. Nothing was too small or too trivial for him: he would sell anything. He was chivied about, insulted, and abused by every one; yet he received it all with a smiling face. Nothing seemed to affect him. He was a typical Japanese, with bright slit-like eyes set as close together as any monkey's--blinking eyes they were, but so intelligent. I could see that he was a keen observer, and that he looked upon these wayfarers as so much material of prey, by the quiet way in which he selected a man with a big pocket, sidling up to him and allowing himself to be insulted, yet always getting the best of the bargain in the end. He tried to sell me some very bad cloisonn? and he was so clever about it, handling his wares in so dexterous a manner,--making his twopenny-halfpenny pots appear of priceless value--that it occurred to me that this little monkey resemblance might have ideas of his own, and be in some small way able to help me. He spoke English a little, and I told him to come up to my room that night, when I should have something to say to him. Glancing at me in a searching way, without asking a single question or showing the slightest surprise, he only said, "I come!"

And he came. When I went up to my room after dinner, I found him sitting there, or rather squatting on a chair, waiting for me, blinking his beady little eyes and looking as solemn as an owl. I told him all my schemes. I explained that I was a painter, thoroughly in sympathy with the Japanese, and that I wanted his help to gather together a company of workers--fan-workers, metal-workers, and screen-workers--in order to furnish a house that I had built in London. He grasped my idea in an instant, and very soon entered into the spirit of the plan, taking an enthusiastic interest in all my schemes. Whenever there was anything that needed measuring exactly, this little man would run his finger and thumb over it in the most dexterous manner possible, murmuring to himself, "One inchie, two inchie, three inchie, seven-and-a-half inchie," etc. I talked on and on, expounding and arranging, until it must have been nearly three o'clock in the morning. Japanese people are in the habit of going to bed very early, and soon my little ally became obviously sleepy, although he was far too polite to admit it. Only when midnight struck did he beg that he might be allowed to smoke a pipe, in order, as he said, "to keep himself awake." I gave him permission, and he immediately jumped into the fireplace, crouching right down in the fender, close up against the red-hot coals, and smoked his miniature pipe there. I talked on, and he listened, really interested in everything I said, and gazing at me with his little beady eyes, bright with interest, yet blinking so rapidly that there was almost a mist over them. Then, for the first time, I noticed that the little soul was tired, and, feeling that it would be cruel to keep him up any longer, I bade him good-night and shut the door.

For almost an hour after he had gone, I sat on dreaming and brooding. Then I was suddenly aroused by hearing a fumbling noise outside my room, as though some one were tapping at the hall door. I went out to see who the intruder might be, and there I found my little Japanese friend, practically asleep, but running his fingers all over the bolted door, trying to measure it, and murmuring, "one inchie, two inchie, three inchie." From that moment I christened him "Inchie," and now all over Japan at the present time this little man is known as Mr. Inchie.

After that night Inchie became my constant companion and friend. Wherever I went he came. Whether it was to theatres, neighbouring towns, metal-workers or fan-workers, Inchie always accompanied me, until in the end it became a daily habit for him to drift about with me in the sunshine, neglecting his business entirely. For Inchie was an artist first and a merchant after. We visited the temples, where Inchie taught me to appreciate the difference between a degenerate Buddha and a perfect Buddha, a difference so subtle as to be quite indistinguishable to the alien. Gradually, bit by bit, as I grew to know him better, this little merchant's true nature revealed itself to me. I began to see the man apart from the merchant, and he proved himself to be a great artist. Here in England we should call him a distinguished genius, and undoubtedly there are scores of equally brilliant men in Japan.

I have indeed no reason to believe that there are any men in Japan who are not brilliant, considering that here, the first man I had met, an ordinary little merchant in a hotel for Europeans, was an artist. Every day we wandered about the streets trying to discover the best operators in metal, wood, and bronze to work for me; and in a very short time we had gathered together a bevy of excellent associates, each thoroughly proficient in his own particular direction.

Inchie and I talked out our plans during our many walks through Uyeno Park and down the theatre streets, and we came to the conclusion that this Japanese house of mine should be a house of flowers. Each room should be some individual and beautiful flower--such as the peony, the camelia, the cherry-blossom, the chrysanthemum,--and, just as a flower begins simply at the base, expanding as it reaches the top into a full-blown bloom, so my rooms should begin with simple one-coloured walls and carpets, becoming richer and richer as they mounted up, ending as they reached the ceiling in a perfect blaze of detail.

That was my dream; but, unlike most dreams, it was realised to the full and far beyond my widest expectations. I first of all turned my attention towards the wood-carvers; and, discovering that each man had his favourite flower, which he manipulated more skilfully than any other, I arranged that he should work solely on that particular species. Having found three or four men who had a special fancy for the peony, I allowed them to occupy themselves entirely in the peony room. I gave them the exact measurement of the ceiling, squaring it out into a certain number of panels, with complete measurements of the doors, the frieze, and every portion of the room, allowing them to give bent to their own artistic instincts as to colour and design. These drawings were then handed over to the wood-carvers, to be pasted on to wood panels and carved. In a very short time every workman in Inchie's store, and every artist too, became enthusiastically interested in this work that they were undertaking. In fact, it was not work to them at all, but one long artistic joy. So much rubbishy bric-a-brac has to be made for the European market that when a Japanese is allowed to go his own way and create self-imagined beautiful things, it is an untold personal pleasure to him.

I never saw a body of men work together so unselfishly as these. The metal-workers in the peony room went on in sympathy with the wood-carvers from the cherry-blossom hall; the screen-makers were interested in the proceedings of the fan-makers; and the designers were interested in them all. Each individual operative was zealously interested in the success of the results as a whole; and the end is that my house now looks like the product of one man, or rather of one master. It was a revelation to me, after my experience of British workmen, to see the way these little Jap fellows toiled. How they would talk and plan out schemes of decoration for me among themselves, studying peony flowers, for instance, in some celebrated temple garden in order to introduce a new and more natural feeling into their wooden ones; and then the joy with which they would think out every little detail, flying round to my hotel at all times of the day to inform me of some new departure, surprised and pleased me greatly.

These men were all brilliant craftsmen and designers, creating work that could not be surpassed in Italy or anywhere else for beauty. Yet the bulk of them were poorly fed, receiving only sevenpence or eightpence a day. Too poor to buy meat, they lived on rice and on the heads and tails of fish twice a week, being unable to afford that which was between.

But although the Japanese workman is very poorly paid, it must also be remembered that his necessities are few and simple. This is roughly the way a workman in Japan lives. He has one meal of rice per day, of the poorest quality, which costs him two sen eight rin. A sen is a tenth part of a penny, and a rin a tenth part of a sen. For a mat to sleep on at night he pays one sen five rin. Three sen he pays for fish or the insides of fowls. Drinking-water costs him two rin, while two rin per day pays for the priest. The total cost of his daily living thus sums up into about five sen three rin. Then, as to be buried at the public expense is considered a deep disgrace, forty sen is always put on one side for the purchase of a coffin, seventy-five sen if the gentleman wishes to be cremated, twenty sen for refreshments for mourners, five rin for flowers, three sen for the fees of the two priests, while, to economise, a Japanese of the lower grade will generally make use of friends as bearers.

Apropos of the absurdly small price at which a man can live in Japan, I am reminded of an experience in Kioto. I was walking down the theatre streets one day with a Japanese friend, and we stopped in front of a little stall full of very dainty toys. There were thousands of toys--miniature kitchen utensils exquisitely carved in wood, small pots and pans and dishes, all bound with lacquer and beautifully finished, such as would delight the heart of every housewife of my acquaintance. I asked the stall-holder, a little stolid old man, through the interpretation of my friend, how much he would sell his entire stock for. His excitement was intense, and my friend told me that my simple question had had the effect of an avalanche upon this stolid little toy-seller, and that he was quite unable to grasp my meaning, so startling and gigantic did the transaction seem to him. After a great deal of gesticulation, and much flicking of the beads on his counting machine, the little man came to the conclusion that his entire stock would be worth two yen thirty sen. This ridiculous price quite took my breath away, and I immediately said that I would buy the lot. Then there was another commotion: the little man was thoroughly upset, and could not understand what I meant. In the end I made him carry away his stall bodily and follow me with it to my hotel. I paid him the money, and he quickly disappeared. "You won't see that little gentleman in theatre street again in a hurry," my friend said: "he will be living in luxury now for a week or more on that two dollar thirty sen, and he certainly won't dream of doing any more work until he has spent the lot." Sure enough, I never saw the stolid toy-seller again during the whole of my stay in Kioto, which stretched over more than a month. But although the coolie and the workman in Japan live on next to nothing, the rich man spends very lavishly. If he entertains you, he gives you a dinner which, although you seldom appreciate its splendid qualities (for it does not appeal to the Western palate), is, from the Japanese standpoint, truly regal. There will be four or five different kinds of fish, some of which will be specimens of great value; and a dinner given at a Japanese tea-house by a merchant to a European friend would cost more than the most expensive dinner it is possible to procure at the Carlton or at the Savoy.

My men flourished on the heads and tails of fish, and did splendid service. Day by day the decorations for my house grew, as one worker after another was added to the little band. One man recommended another, and gradually the number increased, until at last there were as many as seventy working for me Inchie was my help, my interpreter, my foreman. At first there were many difficulties in the way, for Inchie's knowledge of English was limited, and my knowledge of Japanese was none at all. It thus arose that the only method of making him understand me was pantomime. One day, while discussing a certain measurement, we became so involved that I was determined to demonstrate my meaning. So I borrowed the carpenter's tools and constructed a little model of the house, with its different rooms, showing how the carved ceilings and friezes should be placed. Inchie was astounded that I should have so great a knowledge of his own particular work of carpentry, and respected me the more accordingly.

My one great obstacle with the men was in persuading them to make several things alike. They were all artists and hated repeating themselves, and without rhyme or reason I would suddenly find that they had made a red lacquer door twice the size of its fellow by way of variety. When I first employed them I made the grave mistake with my workers of ordering large quantities at a time of required materials. I actually ordered a hundred electric-light fittings--fairy-like lamps daintily wrought in bronze, of which they had made me a model--but they refused me point-blank, and the only way to get them at all was by asking a dozen at a time, and by arranging that each dozen should be varied in some slight respect. It was the same with my picture frames. They were to be a combination of wood and silk, and when I told the master bronze-worker to make me two hundred of them for my next exhibition in London, his face clouded over; he was thoroughly displeased. "No can make," he said decisively: "there is berry much difficulty. Much it cost to make; I must get big shops to do that; I no likee." The little man was quite discouraged, and I was only able to procure my frames by degrees.

Now, in England it would be quite the reverse--the larger the order, the more contented the merchant; but in Japan everything is made by hand. The men take an artistic interest in the work. They hate repeating themselves; and in all the panels designed for my carved ceilings there were not two alike, although the entire design formed a complete whole. Why in the world we do not use Oriental labour in Europe is a marvel to me.

Nothing that these Japanese workmen made for me at the rate of sevenpence or eightpence a day can be approached in London for love or money. I had some gold screens made for me in Japan. They were very beautiful, and were made of gold on silk varnished over and lacquered, with apple-green and vermilion silk borders made from the linings of old dancing dresses. These screens were so brilliant that they were like gold mirrors in which a lady might see her reflection just as accurately as in any Parisian cheval glass. In the passage to England one of the screens became slightly damaged. I was greatly distressed, and took it to a celebrated firm of house-decorators to have it repaired. They undertook the task very confidently; but directly they attempted to match the gold they found that it was impossible to approach to anything like the brilliancy of its surface, although every conceivable method was attempted. They tried putting on gold and then burnishing and varnishing it over to imitate the surface of the lacquer. The result was that, to the present day, that screen stands in my hall with the same dull, sullied patch in the middle of it, a silent testimony to the inferiority of the British house-decorator as compared with his Japanese contemporary.

Little Inchie and I, as I have said, soon became great friends. He followed me about wherever I went, and I often lingered in his store, watching him sell curios to English people and British merchants from Kobe. It was often a revelation to observe the subtlety of the man and the masterly way in which he handled these inquiring visitors. He seemed to divine their inner-most thoughts, and to know at a glance exactly what they wanted, and the prices that they would be likely to pay. After a time I learnt the price of nearly every curio in his store. There was never a fixed value for anything: Inchie was always led by his customer. Perhaps an American and his wife would come in, the man saying nothing, the wife remarking on everything. It was, they said, all "beautiful." I noticed that little Inchie was not at all enthusiastic, merely answering their questions, but not attempting to sell. He would not waste an ounce of energy on them, and after a time they would sweep out of the place, the lady gushing to the last moment and saying how beautiful and exquisite everything was. Directly they had gone I would ask Inchie why he had not worked harder to try and sell them something. "Gentleman and lady not got big pocket," he would say. How in the world he knew that they had but little money puzzled me. "Lady berry much talk--American lady always berry much talk. She say 'This curio number one,' but never buy. English daimio lady come to my store no berry much talk; English gentleman no big pocket. When she leave my store I say, 'Me presentie you.'" What little Inchie means by this is that he feels that this English lady is refined and really admires his beautiful things, but cannot afford to buy them. He appreciates her delicacy, and, in his quaint pidgin English, begs to be allowed the privilege of giving her this little inexpensive trifle to take away.

Very often, when I was spending a morning in Inchie's little curio store, a

Kobe merchant would drop in to buy--a pompous fellow and burly, asking the price of everything he saw. "How much is this? and how much is that?" he would say, and "What do you suppose you'd charge for that?" Inchie would look up at the merchant and blink with almost a scared expression, so meek was it. The merchant, like the great bully that he was, feeling satisfied that he was cowing the little man, would pick up a piece of ivory and say, "How much?" "Four dollars," answers Inchie. "Very dear," replies the merchant sternly. Then Inchie would pick up another piece of ivory, putting away the former, and say with a scared expression, as though the merchant had frightened him down, "I charge two dollars for this." "I will give you one and a half dollar," urges the merchant. And little Inchie, puckering his brow and in a melancholy voice, says, "I takee," the merchant going off highly delighted, convinced that he has been robbing all round.

Immediately after he had left the store, the change in Inchie was extraordinary. He was no longer meek and melancholy, but gleeful and triumphant, and longing to tell me what had happened. "The merchant from Kobe he berry much cheat, that man," he said, with a chuckle. "I show him number one curio, I ask him number one cheap price, and he say, 'Berry dear.' Then I show him no number one curio and ask him more double price. He say, 'I no pay that; I give half that.' He take away curio at half that price, and that very good for me. I make more money like that than when I sell good curio." Then Inchie explained how very easy it is to deceive the average traveller. He does not stand a chance against the Japanese merchant, and half the collections of curios ticketed and placed in museums in England as fine and unique specimens are in reality worthless imitations.

The really fine productions never leave the country at all. Westerners visiting Japan expect to secure fine works of art by paying a small sum for them; but it cannot possibly be done. In that country they know the value of productions, and will not easily part with them. Inchie, becoming very serious and natural, would give me a little lecture on the absurdity of Westerners coming to Japan expecting to buy really fine old curios and pictures at a small price, when no Japanese would part with them for any consideration. "A man," he said, "will come from your country who thinks he understands Japan because he has read some books about it, and has seen some examples of bad art in England. That man has no eyes--he can't see the really beautiful things. He comes to buy the old kakemono. He won't buy the new kakemono by the good man that lives now. He no understand if it good or bad; but it must be old. Well, we make him the old one;" and here Inchie gave me an exact description of how they make the old kakemonos. They first begin by making the paper look old, and every producer has his several methods of bringing about age. This is how Inchie does it. He has eight various stains in eight separate baths, in which he puts his paper, holding the two opposite corners and dashing it from one bath to another in one quick, dexterous sweep. Then the paper is left to dry, and out of about one hundred sheets stained in this way, in all probability only a dozen will be found sufficiently perfect to deceive the buyer. That is the beginning of the manufacture of an imitation old kakemono to be sold to the European connoisseur for hundreds of dollars, afterwards to find its resting-place in some celebrated museum.

What chance has a European against a genius like this? and how can he detect deception in objects that have been the result of such minute care and consideration? The Japanese can imitate postage stamps so accurately that the only hope of discovering a fraud lies in analysing the gum at the back of a stamp. When we stain paper in coffee or beer to give it the effect of age, we consider that we have gone far in the art of imposition; but in this direction, as in many others, we are mere babies compared with the Japanese.

"But then, Inchie," I said, in reply to his statement that it was child's play to deceive the Westerner, "you too are sometimes deceived by us. I know of a gentleman in England who brought over to Japan a large collection of modern porcelain of English manufacture, and by clever handling he imposed the whole lot on an artist at Osaka in exchange for some rare old Satsuma." Then I enlarged on the hardship of the story. I explained how the Englishman had persuaded the Osaka painter to give up all the rare old Satsuma that he had collected during the course of a lifetime in exchange for this valueless English porcelain, remarking that it was wrong and almost cruel to take such a mean advantage of the poor Osaka merchant. "And what do you say to that for a clever fraud, Inchie?" I asked. Inchie only held his sides and laughed. At last he said, "Oh, he berry number one clever man, that at Osaka"; for, it seemed, he knew all about the Englishman and his porcelain, and also about the Satsuma. The painter, indeed, was known all over Japan by his clever imitations of old Satsuma, and it was also generally known that he had given this English gentleman a collection of imitations that he had painted himself in exchange for the English porcelain, which was interesting to him to study. The person to be pitied in Inchie's estimation was the biter bit; and he was "number one sorry for that Englishman."

Whenever any one fresh arrived in Tokio--young, old, pretty, or plain--I always sent him or her to Inchie's store to buy curios. Such streams of people besieged him, all so different and some so quaint, that, although they were good for trade, Inchie was very uncertain as to whether they were good for me, and was anxious to have the matter cleared up. "You have many friends," he would say, eyeing me suspiciously.

At length the crisis was reached which broke down the barriers of Inchie's reserve and thoroughly upset him, in the shape of a fair bulbous woman, who was a terror! I was sitting in the reading-room of the hotel one day, believing that I was alone, when a twangy voice broke in upon the silence. "Just fancy, he shot himself for love of me," mentioning a name in Yokohama. "Really," I observed, feeling embarrassed (he must have been mad, I thought). "Yes; he blew his brains out. Have a drink?" she went on, in an exuberance of generosity. I said, "I think not." She replied that if I would not she would, and she did. She wanted to buy curios. I at once suggested Inchie, which was a happy inspiration. Inchie came round, and I left them in the reading-room together discussing cloisonn?umbrella handles. My companion was lost to me for three full days, being wholly occupied with the fair visitant. He turned up at last, but in a state of fever, his eyes sparkling and blinking indignantly. He handed me a letter that he had just written to his latest customer, my friend the bulbous fair, who had left for Shanghai that day. "You order me much porcelain; you order me many curios; I no can send. I think you better go porcelain Yokohama. Much cheaper you get Yokohama, more number one," Inchie's letter ran. "Yes; but, Inchie," I remonstrated, "why won't you serve her? She's a good customer for you." He was violent with rage. "I no like the lady," he said; "she no daimio lady. Tea-house lady, I think, with tea-coloured hair. She received me with not a proper dress on; she smoke and drink. I no want to serve lady like that. She no friend of yours?" he added, eagerly looking into my face with his piercing little eyes. "No, no, Inchie! of course not," I replied, for I wasn't going to claim her. "Ah, I thought she no friend of yours," and Inchie smiled, while I felt that I was respected once more and entered into his good graces--it turned out for ever.

"Now, Inchie," I said to him one day, "I want to get a good porcelain man, the best in Tokio. Can you manage it?" There was nothing, so far as I knew, that Inchie could not manage, so that in a very short time he had found a little man, a pupil of the most eminent porcelain maker in Tokio, also celebrated for his remarkable glazes, who had just started a business of his own. We drove round to his store to ask him if he would undertake the painting of a dinner-service, and do other things for me. He was a young man, this particular painter, but with the face of a very old one, careworn and haggard, quite an enthusiast, full of interest in his art, and a craftsman of the highest order. When he found that I too was in the same ranks, his sympathies were aroused, and he devoted a whole month solely to the firing and painting of my porcelain. After a time I began to understand the man and his processes. He brought out little bits of choice Chinese-blue porcelain to show me. Whenever there was to be a three-days' firing he would come round to my hotel and inform me of it. Altogether he developed into quite a friend, almost to the dethronement of Inchie. He allowed me to sit among the men while they worked, and, seeing how interested I was, they gave me some clay to model and paint. I ended by painting a whole dinner-service in blue and white. It took me a week to do; but it was perhaps one of the most delightful experiences I have ever had, and I can safely say that I have never worked in a more congenial atmosphere than when sitting on a mat in that little porcelain shop surrounded by those twelve little artists. I shall never forget the anxious moments when my products were being fired. Sometimes

I have gone on for twelve or fourteen hours, eating and resting with the men, taking my turn at keeping the furnace alight, and hanging about after the kilns had cooled to see my valuable porcelain dug out.

Nothing can be more exciting than the first peep at porcelain after it has been fired. A mass of dead heavy-looking clay is put into the furnace and fired; you peep at it after some hours, and find, to your surprise, a rare paradise of glazed white and blue, so brilliant and sparkling that it seems almost impossible to have been made by mortal hands. But then, of course, it is not always so delightful; there are sometimes vexing surprises awaiting you as you open the oven door. Occasionally you will peep in and see a group of vases looking like drunken men lolling against one another in a disreputable manner, and lurching over at all angles. Surrounded by a series of failures such as these, the finest work is almost invariably found. Although the vases have all been painted by the same hand and fired in the same kiln, only one will be perfect, while the rest are worthless. This is probably brought about by some subtle influence to be found in the placing of the vase in the kiln. There is, however, a great deal of uncertainty in such operations, and it is almost impossible to foretell the fate of any piece of ware after it has been set in the firing kiln.

Inchie and I spent much of our time with the bronze-workers, and it amused me to see these artists carrying out designs for the European market, while to hear their comments upon the crude productions of Englishmen was sometimes very funny indeed.

The men who were thus engaged were at the same time carrying out exquisite work for me. They complained that the European market insisted upon everything being over-elaborated and very showy, and at the same time very old. This combination is quite impossible. The old Japanese bronze work was always very simple in design, depending for its beauty, not upon the flowery decorations surrounding it, but upon the exquisite proportions of the piece itself. To create the aged appearance necessary in the eyes of the faddy European, the bronzes have to be buried in the earth--in a special kind of earth--for a few days; after which they are dug up and sold to connoisseurs and English people, who are by way of understanding works of art, for fabulous sums.

I had occasion to employ many embroiderers; and here, as in every other branch of Japanese art work, I received a series of "eye-openers." Hitherto I had been envious of the many fine old bits of embroidery and temple hangings shown me by the different globe-trotters staying at the hotel. They had all come upon their treasures in some lucky and unexpected manner. By much good fortune every man had secured his own special piece of embroidery, and each by clever manipulation had outwitted the dealer from whom he had managed to wrest this one old temple hanging. But when I went to headquarters, and began to employ the men who actually made the fabric, my envy vanished. I soon found that none of these coveted treasures was old at all. Such large pieces of embroidery are not used in temples, nor have they ever been; they are quite modern introductions, and have been brought about simply to attract and make money out of the credulous strangers. I have spent hour after hour with the embroiderers, watching them manipulate old temple hangings, and have seen them when the task was over wash on gold stains with base metal. Here and there a few little touches would be of real gold, and it was all done so cleverly that none but a Jap could possibly detect that they were modern.

It is almost a depressing sight to watch these embroiderers at work--so different are they from the happy boisterous metal-workers talking and laughing amid the clanging of their little hammers. They are sad and silent. You will be in a roomful of these people for perhaps a whole morning, and not one of them will utter a word. They work on and on, with heads bent down, picking up thread after thread of the one piece of embroidery that they have been constantly working on for months, or perhaps for years. Never a word nor a smile; each peering into his own special work with painful red eyes, on which are large bone-rimmed spectacles. They all, as a rule, lose their sight early in thus poring incessantly over this difficult and dainty work.

I ordered several pieces of cotton cr雅 e of a certain design that I had drawn myself, and it was during the execution of this commission that I was brought into touch with the stencil-workers and dyers of the country. Stencil-cutting is one of the most beautiful arts imaginable. To see the stencil-workers cutting fantastic designs from the hard polished cardboard beneath their instruments--so delicate that it is like the tracery of a spider's web in its tenuity--is a sight that one never forgets. Some of the designs are so cobweb-like that single human hairs are used in parts to keep them from breaking to pieces.

Dyeing is also an art that is brought to a high degree of perfection in Japan. Sometimes an elaborate design will need such a large number of plates and colours, as well as finishing touches by the hand of the operator, that in the end it looks almost like a water-colour, so closely do the colours mingle one with another.

Then there were the carpenters, and here a whole series of surprises awaited me. For example, I found that the teeth of their saws were set in what may be called the opposite direction, and that therefore, when a man pulled his instrument towards him, it cut the wood, rather than when he pushed. In this, as in everything else, the Japanese are perfectly right. One always has more strength to pull than to push, and with this method you are enabled to use saws made of such thin metal that if their teeth were set in the opposite direction they must needs cockle and break. When a carpenter wants to plane some tiny piece of wood, perhaps a portion of a miniature doll's house, he does not run a small plane over it, as we do, but uses a large heavy one, very sharp, and turned upside-down. In this way very delicate work can be achieved.

All the Japanese tools are designed with a view to their special fitness. The chisels work in a totally different way from that of our chisels, and lend themselves more readily to delicate work. As to their little wood-carving tools, they are perfect joys! I shall never forget the expressions on the faces of my British workmen as they unpacked the cases of goods that arrived from Japan, and came across saws as thin as tissue paper with their teeth set the wrong way; tiny chisels that almost broke as they handled them; hammers the size of a lady's hat-pin. My foreman's face was a study of disgusted contempt. "Now, how can a man turn out decent work with tools like that?" he exclaimed, looking round appealingly. And it did seem impossible. But not one of them complained when they came across the actual work accomplished by these ridiculously small instruments. The carpenters were loud in their admiration for the wood-carving, and the foreman merely sniffed. He knew that he himself could not approach it. And this was soon clearly proved, for if ever my hands tried to do a bit of patching it was always a failure. All their joining was as child's play when compared with this Japanese triumph.

There was a man in Osaka, a perfect genius in wood-carving--the king of carpenters. People journeyed from long distances to pay their respects to him, and he was the most independent person I ever saw in my life. He never dreamt of undertaking service for people unless they appreciated it and understood its value. Very rich Americans have tried to persuade him to engage for them; but, as he always demanded that would-be purchasers should be capable of appreciating his work as that of an accomplished artist, they rarely ever succeeded. Nearly all this man's work is done for his own people at a very low price, and Japanese wood-carvers are continually taking pilgrimages to see him and to buy specimens of his productions. He always demands to know what is going to become of them, and where they are going to be placed, before consenting to part with them. I had the wit not to ask him to sell anything to me, nor to execute anything for me, but simply admired his work as that of a unique artist.

Most prominent among the toilers of Japan are the workers in lacquer, clean and dainty beyond description, with whom a great portion of my time was taken up. The climate of the country is exactly suited to the making of lacquer, being sufficiently damp. The process is unusually elaborate, and is a tedious matter of painting on a very large number of coats of lacquer, rubbing them down always, and allowing them to dry. When we think of lacquer here in

England, we think of it in connection with our tea-trays and like cheap goods which we complain of as being made of bad material that chips and breaks and becomes useless in a distressingly short space of time. "The Japanese have lost the art of creating the fine old lacquer that they used formerly," we say. But it is not so at all; it is purely a question of time. If the Japanese were allowed sufficient leisure, and were not rushed on so by the requirements of the European market, they would be able to turn out just as fine and just as durable lacquer as they did in the days when they worked for the love of their work alone for purchase by their fellow-countrymen. Practical proof of this can be found in the fact that all the doors in my London house, which are composed of the best lacquer, twenty or thirty coats thick, and have been in constant use for years, are still in perfect condition, and will be two hundred years hence. One has no idea before going to Japan of the extensive range of colours in the way of greens, blues, and reds that there is in lacquer, for most of the colours are entirely unknown in the West. There is undoubtedly no surface in the world that is as clear and as brilliant as lacquer, and I have often thought how advantageous it would be if one could only lacquer pictures over instead of varnishing them; it would give to the poorest work a brilliancy and crispness that would be simply invaluable. But this brilliant surface is only brought about by excessive care and cleanliness in its preparation--indeed, it needs almost as much attention as the making of a collotype plate.

I was anxious to get some really good cloisonn?workers to make some things for me, and by very good luck I hit upon a man who had just discovered an entirely new method of handling gold. Coming across one of his samples at an exhibition in Tokio, I ferreted him out and persuaded him to engage for me. His cloisonn? unlike the ordinary slate-grey work that one must needs peer closely into before discovering its fine qualities, was bold in design, with flower patterns of cherry-blossom just traceable through a fine lacework of gold, and it looked like a brilliant rainbow-hued bubble. One is much inclined to fancy that cloisonn?vases with elaborate designs must necessarily be expensive. That, however, is not the case. There are technical obstacles connected with making broad sweeps of colour in cloisonn?that render simple designs much more expensive. Japan is the only place in the world that is capable of producing cloisonn? for the patience and skill required would overtax the workers of any other country, and such an attempt would necessarily end in failure. A cloisonn?shop is every bit as depressing as the embroidery works. You will see men picking up on the end of their tiny instruments gold wire, which is so microscopic as to be like a grain of dust, and almost as invisible. This tiny morsel has to be placed on the metal vase and fixed there.

Talking of the delicate and exquisite tools used by cloisonn?workers reminds me of tools that are just as delicate, but used for quite another purpose-- namely, those which the Japanese dentists handle so dexterously. However, the stock-in-trade of a Japanese dentist chiefly consists of the proper use of his finger and thumb. The most strongly-rooted tooth invariably gives way to this instrument. A Japanese dentist has only to apply his fingers to a tooth, and out that tooth comes on the instant. It is sometimes very amusing to see a group of dentists' assistants, all mere children, practising their trade by endeavouring to pull nails out of a board, beginning with tin tacks and ending with nails which are more firmly rooted than the real teeth themselves.

When I had gathered my team together by the help of my right-hand ally, Inchie, after having chosen the best of them from every branch of art, they continued to go on well and assiduously, and the decorations of my house were in full swing, when suddenly there was a break, a distinct break. I went round to the store early one lovely morning in May, as was my habit, and found, to my surprise, that the whole place was empty. Not a metal-worker or carpenter was to be seen. They had all mysteriously disappeared--where? To view the cherry-blossom! Inchie also, whom I had relied upon as a good steady colleague, had, on the first opportunity, and without any warning, drifted away into the open air with the whole band to view the blossom. The Japanese workmen, who are skilled, and want examples from Nature, evidently adhere to the principle that "all work and no play makes Jack a dull boy," and so, whether I liked it or not, when such a glorious day had presented itself, they were not going to miss the opportunity of enjoying it. It was a holiday, or rather the sunshine had declared it to be a holiday, and all Japan, rich and poor, employers and employed, had turned out to picnic in the parks, and feast their eyes upon the cherry-blossom. So universal was the holiday, and so persistently did Inchie implore that I should join them, that I soon found myself sitting under the trees in Uyeno Park, surrounded by my deserters, enjoying things as well as any one of them there.

It was on this day, out of the pure joy of the idea, that Inchie proposed to give me a real Japanese dinner, and at the same time show me some of the fine old classical dances of Japan. I remember that night so well! Inchie invited three other Japanese friends, and we all went down into the basement with rod and line, or, to be exact, with a net, to catch our own fish for dinner. It was to me novel sport chasing those lazy old goldfish round the tank. I secured a monster, which beat Inchie's out and out for size. Inchie was in splendid form on this occasion; it was a field-night for him, and he was quite at his best. He was an enormous eater; he ate anything you chose to give him, and he enjoyed the dinner that followed our half-hour spent below stairs, I must confess, far more than I did. For although the repast was of the very best quality, it was after all Japanese, which statement speaks for itself, as every one knows that Japanese food does not by any means commend itself to the British palate. There was our just-caught fish cooked with bamboo, meat of different sorts, and many varieties in the soup character, some of which were not bad. As for the Sake, it tasted like bad sherry; but it had a most exhilarating effect on Inchie, and in a very short time produced in him a most natural and joyous frame of mind which enabled me to see a side of his disposition that under ordinary conditions would never have come to the surface. One of the courses of this dinner of dinners was a chicken, provided out of deference to my European tastes, and Inchie carved it. It was a muscular bird; but Inchie carved it with a pair of large chopsticks as I have never seen a chicken carved before in any part of the globe. Not even Joseph of the Savoy with his flourish of fork and knife in mid-air could compete with Inchie and his pair of wooden chopsticks. No knives nor fingers were used; but the whole was limbed, cut up, and served in less than the period that Joseph would take in his skilled dexterity.

I remarked upon his skill in handling the chopsticks, and Inchie at once suggested that we should all have a competition to see who could pick up the greatest amount of peas with chopsticks in the shortest possible time. Each was given a lacquer tray with carefully numbered green peas, cold and cooked--the number according to the proficiency of the player. Inchie's plate was loaded; the guests and geishas had a fair amount; but I had only three, and the aim was to pick them up one by one and put them into our mouths, the competitor whose plate was empty first being declared the winner. We started, and I was so intent on the manipulation of my three green peas that I was only conscious of a whirl of hands, never having noticed that the rest had finished their pile before I had picked up my second pea. I never undertook such a task before, nor ever will again. The discouragement of it was final. My first pea, after no little exertion and much sleight of hand, I had raised to my lips on the points of the chopsticks, when just at the critical moment it abruptly left its moorings, went like a shot from a catapult across the room, and settled itself on the lap of one of the geishas, who was thereby promptly put out of the contest. I do not know what happened to the second pea, much less of the fate of the third; all I remember is that I came in a very bad last in the chopstick competition.

What with the Sake, the competition, and the dinner, Inchie became more and more brilliant, until at last an idea sparkled out that was worthy of his distinction. I was to have a piece of wood-carving in my London house that should be as it were the eye of the peacock--the first ever made in Japan! We should go to Osaka together, he remarked, the very next day, choose a great piece of wood 8 or 9 feet in length, 3 feet broad, and about 6 inches through, and have it carved in the most beautiful and magnificent chrysanthemum pattern ever seen--for the hall was of chrysanthemums. His eyes sparkled as he said, "You are going to have berry number one house; must have one big number one piece chrysanthemum carving--better than any other carving, better than temple carving." The Sake passed round, the geishas danced, and Inchie talked, while with every cup he grew brighter and brighter, and his eyes sparkled like jewels. I was beginning to see the real Inchie. Was this really the little man, the laughing-stock of the hotel, bullied and sworn at by every one? He talked of Hookosai, who, he asserted, was not the great master that he is universally considered to be in Europe. Hookosai was too realistic; many other artists were far finer. Yet another cup of Sake was passed round and drained. "I will demonstrate some Hookosai pictures," said little Inchie, in a tone of suppressed excitement; and, stepping behind a screen as he spoke, reappeared almost immediately with a handkerchief rolled round his head and his kimono tucked up, posing in the attitude of one of the most celebrated of Hookosai's pictures. Twenty or thirty pictures were represented, and in each he was a different man merely by changing the muscles of his face. Never have I seen such acting in my life; he was like a gallery of Hookosai's pictures rolled into one, with all their queer exaggeration.

More Sake was drunk, and later in the evening Inchie became so excited that, in order to work off his condition, he made the remarkable proposal that he should show me a devil dance. When he emerged from behind the screen, the geishas were frightened and drew back in alarm; for he was no longer the gentle little monkey merchant, but a real devil. As for the dancing, I never saw anything so superbly fine! It almost took my breath away. He seemed almost superhuman, an ethereal creature.

The evening ended up in the usual way. Next morning Inchie came round to my hotel, sat down on a chair looking amazingly sheepish, and blinked solemnly at me. "Well, what's up now, Inchie?" I inquired, seeing that he had something to say. "Berry number one bad night last night, Sir," moaned Inchie with a shake of his head. "I no want you to tell people I do the devil dance last night. They no understand and berry much talk. Please, I beg you not tell!" And poor little Inchie went about for days with a drooping head, looking the picture of misery. But in my opinion, he had no reason to be ashamed of his conduct; he had shown himself to be a versatile genius. He had acted as I never before have seen a man act; he had also danced as I have never seen a man dance; and he had drunk as I have never seen a man drink without becoming badly affected. Nevertheless, this was the man who had allowed himself, and was allowing himself, to be sworn at, bullied, and even kicked by the common sorts and by the vulgar globe-trotters.

The day following the night of the never-to-be-forgotten dinner, Inchie and I went, as we had intended, to Osaka to choose a fine and sufficiently well-seasoned piece of wood for this famous and all-important wood-carving, the eye of the peacock. I think we must have visited every timber-yard in Osaka in search of a fitting plank, and it was too funny to see the way Inchie would crawl over a piece of wood, like the small monkey that he was, scratching, rubbing, picking it with his nail, and even putting his tongue upon it to test its quality. At last a plank was found that was declared to be "berry number one," and the great undertaking, the work of carving it, began. Five men were at work on it for five months. And now that it is completed and fixed in my chrysanthemum hall, it is a triumph! It is a joy--it is a possession! At the same time, when we were in Osaka, Inchie was struck with another brilliant idea. I must have a gong, he said, a superb gong; and as Inchie himself had once been a metal-worker, he was an excellent judge of gongs and undertook to choose one for me. Before that day I had no notion that there could be such a vast difference in gongs. We went to about twenty or thirty stores in Osaka, at each of which several gongs were produced for our inspection. And Inchie bounded about the shop like a cat or a leopard, from one corner of the room to the other, crouching down on the ground with his hand over his ear, striking each in turn, and listening to its vibration. "No berry good that," he would whisper to me, and then, talking charmingly to the merchant,--for Inchie was always charming--he would bow himself gracefully out of the shop. At each store in turn the same thing happened, until at last we reached a shop which seemed to me still more improbable than the rest, for it was a dirty little hole of a place, with no such thing as a gong in sight. In reply to our usual question the proprietor dived into a tangled bit of garden at the back, and presently reappeared with an old rusty gong, very thin with age and use and exposure to all weathers, and looking not worth twopence. Inchie struck it, and the expression on his face was extraordinary as he looked round at me. The tone was superb. This was the gong of gongs! "That berry number one," he exclaimed in a stage whisper. We secured the gong for a few cents. "Big-pockety man no berry clever, I think," remarked Inchie pensively.

It was on the day of my last visit to his store before sailing for England, and Inchie was very sad, very earnest, and very anxious to give me the best possible advice as to what to do in the way of selling when I arrived at my "store," as he termed it, in England. "When big-pocket man come to Japan, every merchant know, and all wait for him," said Inchie, by way of demonstrating to me how very easy it was to entrap a rich man into buying one's goods. Inchie also told me the following story of how two big-pockety men once fared at the hands of a very subtle merchant. He was a Tokio merchant, and directly he heard of their probable arrival he sent experienced guides to almost every port in Japan to waylay these arrivals. They were eventually caught at Kobe, and were led all over Japan by a remarkably efficient guide, in due course reaching Tokio. After visiting many curio stores they were safely landed at the store of the master exactor. Then the trickery developed. The merchant began to flatter and compliment the richer of the two, and knowing that they were anxious to buy gold lacquer he said: "You are a great connoisseur on gold lacquer, I believe. They tell me that you have a quick eye for fine work, and I have heard much of your appreciation of Japanese art." The big-pockety man was thus won over into a limp and restful condition, for no one can flatter to such good advantage as the Japanese.

Meantime the guide was walking about the shop with his mouth wide open and looking silly. He was there to protect the two men, and the keenest observer could never have guessed that he was in reality the agent of this merchant. "I want your guide to take you round to all the gold lacquer shops you can, for I know that that is what you appreciate and love so much. After you have seen all that the merchants can show you, come back to me and see what you think of my specimens." All this time he was toying with a little insignificant-looking gold lacquer tray, turning it about under the rich man's very nose in such a way that he was bound to notice it. "We Japanese are so clever, you know, and we are such good imitators of lacquer that even I, a Japanese, am liable at times to be misled by some of the deceptions. But," continued the merchant in an off-hand manner, "there is one sure test of real gold lacquer, and that is the fire test." So saying he carelessly lit a match and allowed it to play all over the gold lacquer tray; then quietly and without any demonstration he handed it to the rich man and begged him to observe that it was not harmed in any way, taking it for granted that he, the rich man, naturally knew of the fire test.

The big-pocket man puckered his fat brow critically--he really knew nothing about it--and rubbed his greasy palm over the surface of the lacquer. The difference between the hands of the two men was a characteristic study--one big and flabby, the other slim and sinuous with fingers that almost turned back in their energy. After examining the tray closely the visitor admitted that it was in truth untouched. The master exactor smiled, and, like the rogue he was, never referred to it again. The two rich men went away with their guide and visited half a dozen other stores in Tokio, trying the fire test on all the gold lacquer they could find, with disastrous consequences.

They had to pay for damages wherever they went, and wherever they went the merchants were indignant, for real gold lacquer, as every one knows, will not stand such treatment unless it happens to be a flat tray. But the rich men only chuckled at their superior knowledge and paid the damages without a murmur. Then they went back to the store of the evil prompter and did exactly as he expected they would do; they bought ten thousand pounds' worth of gold lacquer, all of which was "berry number one imitation gold lacquer," as Inchie remarked. "Well, but, Inchie, I couldn't treat people like that." I told the little man "I shouldn't know how." "But I will show you how to sell," quoth Inchie: "I show you how to sell two-cent blue porcelain pot in your store for two hundred dollars to big-pockety man"; whereupon Inchie proceeded to give me a lesson in the art of selling. He first brought out a nest of six lacquer boxes that fitted one into the other; then he held up the two-cent porcelain pot,--and the way he handled it made it already begin to appear valuable in my eyes. I truly believe that Inchie could stroke out a piece of newspaper and make it seem as rare as a bank-note. Then this little genius wrapped the worthless blue porcelain in yellow silk, and placed it in the smallest lacquer box, which with its lid he secured inside a larger box, and so on until the entire six boxes and their lids encased his gem. Placing it upon the table, he began to explain how I should sell it, and in order to describe the subtlety of the transaction I must give it in Inchie's own words: "Big-pockety man come your store in England and he say, 'Mr. Menpes, you bought number one curio in Japan?' You say, 'No buy curio in Japan,' but you talk much to him of all the beautiful things you see in Japan. After a time you look on the ground and think--much you show you think. Big-pockety man look at you and he no talk. You look up quick and you say, 'Oh, number one curio I buy Japan, I remember!' He say, 'Please show me curio.' 'Never I show curio,' you tell him. 'I buy number one curio, but I no want to show.' Then you talk to him about Japan, all the streets and the theatres you see in Japan; but all the time he talk of curio--'I ber-ry much want to see,' he say. You say, 'You friend, you number one friend? Very well, I show.'" After having thus given way you must go upstairs and look for the curio, and--Inchie laid a stress upon this last statement--"you must be a long time finding it. When you come back you place the large lacquer box containing the five smaller boxes and the Buddha's eye--the Holy of Holies--upon the table, and much you begin to talk about Japan, berry like American lady talk I think; you no talk to him then about porcelain. After much talk about beautiful blossom you take out one box; then you talk more and take out another box--gentleman he ber-ry much want to see. When you come to final piecee box he berry much excited, and when you take out the porcelain and yellow silk you berry berry quiet--no artistic to talk now. Then you drop the corners of the silk and look at the porcelain. You no talk, big-pockety man no talk; he no understand this--berry funny. Somebody must talk, all quiet; you rest long time no talk, and big-pockety man say, 'Berry much number one curio that I think--how much you sell?' You say, 'I no sell. Berry much money that costee me Japan, much ricksha, much hotel. Number one Chinese porcelain that. Number one glaze. I no sell,'" And to cut the story short I must explain that "the big-pockety man"--that is the millionaire--is by this time in a perfect fever to possess my priceless blue porcelain, and, Inchie says, here I must weaken, and after asking him if he is "daimio gentleman number one," I must allow him to buy my two-cent vase for two hundred dollars.

In giving me this important lesson in the art of selling, Inchie considered that he had shown me the truest mark of friendship, and that he had given me the most valuable present in his power, and far more useful than any jewel could be.

Towards the end of the work, when the house was nearly completed, and I had entertained mentally almost every friend I knew, and had missed nothing from the door-mat to the red lacquer soup-bowls on the dining-room table, I suddenly remembered the door-knocker. There was no door-knocker! I immediately interviewed Inchie and asked him to help me to design a door-knocker. Seeing that the only doors they have in Japan are sliding ones made of tissue paper, it was some time before Inchie could comprehend my meaning. "I no understand why you want to knock at the door. Very funny that!" he said. I explained that in England it was necessary to have very strong doors which one could not leave open lest people should come in and steal. He blinked his little eyes and looked up at me intelligently: "I understand!" he exclaimed, "berry number one bad Chinaman come and steal." "No," I said, "not Chinaman, but Englishman." "I no understand," he repeated. After much pantomime and talk I at last conveyed to him a fairly good idea of what was needed in the way of a door-knocker, and sent him home to work out some suitable design. Three days after he came back carrying under his arm a huge roll of drawings, which he proceeded to unfold on the floor. A glance was enough to show me that the little fellow had not got hold of the kind of door-knocker I required, and I watched him with a limp and hopeless feeling. "Go on, Inchie: explain it," I said. He was in very good condition this morning-- pleased with himself and the world in general, and more especially with his door-knocker design. Drawing in his breath with a little satisfied hiss, he began: "Now, you see, you first put on the door a large chrysanthemum in bronze," and Inchie went through the performance in pantomime. "In the centre of this chrysanthemum a rod of steel must be fixed five inches in length. Suspended from the rod of steel must be a silk cord about five inches in length, and attached to the cord a marble about the size of a child's playing marble. Underneath the large chrysanthemum, and in line with the marble, should be placed another chrysanthemum with a miniature gong in the centre three-quarters of an inch in diameter." "Wait a bit, Inchie," I cried, for this description was too much for me--I must digest it more slowly. I pictured to myself the strings of children that pass and repass my house in Cadogan Gardens on their way to and from school, and their feelings concerning this small metal ball waving in the soft wind of a summer's afternoon on its apple-green cord. It would be too gorgeous an attraction by far! No child could have the heart to destroy so rare a thing at once, it would be far too great a joy; they would save it at least until their return journey from school before even touching it. Seeing that the small man was becoming a little offended, I said, "Fire away, Inchie,--what next?" "Well, when you come home after dinner, you take the marble and hold it five inches from the gong. You shut one eye and take aim; then you let go, and he goes ping! ping! and gentleman he come and open the door." "No, he doesn't, Inchie," I shouted: "you're wrong there--the gentleman doesn't open the door." "I no understand," said little Inchie, his face falling,--"why he no open the door?" "Because," I explained, "when you come home late at night after dinner you must have very sure habits of taking aim in order to strike that miniature gong three-quarters of an inch in diameter." Inchie looked up at me with bright pathetic little eyes, and said, "Berry fine daimio door-knocker this, and it is not difficult for you to strike. I no understand!" Then I took him on one side, not wanting to hurt his feelings, and explained to him how almost impossible it would be for a man coming home after dinner, having walked hurriedly and all that, to take aim at his miniature gong. "You told me you could shoot a rifle," was Inchie's reply. After that there was no more to be said, for I realised that one must necessarily be a rifle shot before you could get home at nights.

The last I ever saw of poor little Inchie was when he came on board the P. and O. steamer at Yokohama to see me off on my journey to England. The authorities would not allow him to lunch with me in the saloon, and the poor little fellow, who was far more refined and certainly had far more intelligence than any one on board, captain and officers included, was compelled to eat his luncheon standing up in the steward's pantry, which hurt his feelings terribly. The only figure that I seemed to see in the mist that enwrapped Yokohama wharf was poor little Inchie standing there in his blue kimono and quaint bowler hat, watching me with eager blinking eyes that had a suspicion of moisture about them, and lips that twitched slightly; and the last thing I heard was, "I think when you go to England you send me berry many letters-- often you send me." And I felt as the steamer moved away that I had lost a good and a true friend.

When the decorations for my house arrived in London, the next and all important question to be considered was how to put them up. Everything was finished and ready to fix in its place without nails, and the only thing left to be completed by the British workmen was the slight wooden beams and square framework in which the carved panels were to be fixed. I secured five or six good workmen, and literally taught them how to handle this material, but it took them two years to put up what my Japanese craftsmen had produced in one year. It was all straightforward clean design, and there was no artistic effort needed for it; but the obstacle was that they always struggled to make the woodwork a little thicker than necessary. Their inclinations were always to strengthen things, and it took a great deal of perseverance and patience to uproot their fixed ideas. Then I had a great deal of trouble with the painters. At first they almost refused to put distemper on my walls. Strings upon strings of painters I was compelled to dismiss because they would persist in putting what they called "body" into the paint. Sometimes they would slip it in behind my back; but I always detected it and dismissed the men on the instant. It was the only way. "Well, I've been in the trade for thirty years and I've always used body"--they all said that, and every workman I have ever employed, or is yet to be employed, always says the same. No matter how young or how old they may be, they have always been in the trade for thirty years. One painter I educated sufficiently to allow of him going so far against his principles as to leave out "body," but when I ordered him to mix oil and water by beating them together in a tub he declined and left. The only men whom I was able to persuade to do this for me were my foreman and one of the carpenters. The foreman was a very intelligent little man, whom I had educated to such an extent that his views of life and of workmen in general were entirely changed. He sneered at them, and was altogether so won over to my ideas that I am afraid I totally destroyed him for any other work. The painter, on the other hand, had no intelligence at all, but was equally devoted, and I feel quite sure that those two poor operatives are drifting about now doing anything but their respective trades of carpentry and painting. They undertook the beating of the oil and water very energetically, and kept it up for days, relieved occasionally by the caretaker. Eventually the oil did mix, and the experiment was a great success. Towards the end of their training these men became so accustomed to looking at things, if not feeling them, from the decorative standpoint, that it was no unusual occurrence to overhear such remarks as the following. The foreman would say to his pal as he caught sight of the reflection of his grimy face in a mirror: "I say, Bill, my flesh tone looks well against this lemon yellow, don't it?" or "I suppose I must start and wash off this toney"--toney meaning dirt, but to call it dirt would be to their enlightened minds vulgar in the extreme. Everything with them was "tone."

A few days before they left for good I overheard a conversation between Bill and his mate, who had begun to feel the hopelessness of attempting work of a different nature. "What shall we do, Bill, when this blooming job's over?" said the foreman. "I suppose we shall go a-'opping!" replied Bill. It was then just about the hopping season.

CHARACTERISTICS

CHAPTER XI

CHARACTERISTICS

Perhaps one of the most admirable features in the character of the Japanese is their great power of self-control. The superficial observer on his first visit to Japan, because of this very quality of theirs, is at first liable to imagine that the Japanese have no emotion. This is a mistake. I have lived with them; I know them through and through; and I know that they are a people of great emotions, emotions that are perhaps all the deeper and stronger because they are unexpressed. Self-control is almost a religion with the Japanese. In their opinion it is wrong and selfish to the last degree to inflict one's sorrows and one's cares upon other people. The world is sad enough, they argue, without being made sadder by the petty emotions of one's neighbour: so the people of Japan all contrive to present a gay and happy appearance to the outside world. You may express your feelings in the solitude of your own room, and there is no doubt that the Japanese suffer terribly among themselves, although a stranger, and especially a European, will never detect a trace of it.

I once went to call, with a resident of Japan, on an old Japanese lady, to condole with her on the loss of her husband and her only son, who had both been swept away, with thousands of others, in a great tidal wave only a few days previously. As we neared the house we saw, through the partially-opened sliding door, the old woman rocking herself to and fro in an agony of sorrow, literally contending with emotion, and suffering as I have never seen a human being suffer before. I was terribly shocked, and we naturally hesitated for some time before announcing ourselves; but by the time the mourner appeared at the door to greet us, she was all smiles. It was difficult to believe that she was the same woman. Her face shone with radiant happiness, and all traces of sorrow had disappeared. In the course of the conversation she did not avoid the sore subject, but rather chose it, and talked of the death of her husband and her son with a smiling face and an expression by which one might very pardonably have judged that she had no feelings whatever. This was self-control indeed, and it is only in Japan that one encounters such striking illustrations of superb pluck and endurance.

In my opinion, this great self-control is an evidence of the very high standard of civilisation of the Japanese. If one is at all observant and really in sympathy with the people, one is continually catching glimpses of their real natures and instances of their magnificent self-command. Once I was talking to a little Japanese merchant, along with some friends whom I had taken round to his store to buy curios. I had made quite a friend of this man, and knew him well. We were all chaffing him about getting married, and one of my friends said to him, "Well, why don't you get married? But perhaps you have already got a wife!" The little man looked up quickly with a smile on his face, and said--"Me married already; me wife die two years past; two children die two years past; all die, I think." The voice was perfectly steady, and the face smiling, as he uttered this amazingly sad statement; but some one chanced to look up and saw two great tears standing in his little monkey-like eyes. Of course he was "no class," and, not being an actual workman, but only a merchant, he was considered to be of rather a low grade. Still, for this slight show of emotion, he had utterly disgraced himself in his own eyes, and would afterwards, no doubt, atone for it by torturing himself in private.

I saw many remarkable instances of the self-control of the Japanese people when I visited the scenes of desolation caused from that great tidal wave which destroyed nearly three thousand people. Village after village I visited, some of them with only three or four living inhabitants left; but in no case, with men, women, or children, did I see the slightest trace of emotion. Here and there, indeed, you passed a woman huddled up in a corner muttering and screaming, but only because her mind had become unhinged by the loss of her home, or probably village, and every relation she possessed. No Japanese in his senses would amid the same circumstances be guilty of so much as a murmur or a tear.

The Japanese are a brave people--not only the men, but the women too. In fact, the women more especially are brave. Many women destroyed themselves during the China-Japanese war, because their husbands had been killed in battle. There was one Japanese woman in Tokio who felt so deeply the disgrace placed upon her country by the attempt on the life of the present Emperor of Russia some years ago by a common coolie, that she committed suicide. She felt that this great European prince had visited her country as a guest, and that before Japan could raise its head once more the nation must make some great sacrifice. Day after day she visited the Legation, and begged to be allowed admission to some of the high officials--in vain: they were too busy to see her. At last, after some weeks of fruitless effort, she went home in despair and killed herself, leaving a pathetic little letter to the Minister stating that she hoped that the sacrifice of her life might in some way help to cleanse her country from its disgrace.

Patriotism is a strong trait in the character of the Japanese; but perhaps their imagination and their love of Nature are even stronger, and at all events will cause them to bound forward and become a first-rate power. This universal force of the imagination is a quality that no other nation possesses, and it is a quality that will cause her, not so very many years hence, to dominate the world. All the Japanese possess imagination, from the highest to the lowest; it is shown in every action and detail of their daily life. There is no one of them, even to the poorest coolie, who has not some little collection of exquisite works of the art that he loves. Your jinricksha man, if you were ever allowed the privilege of visiting his house, would in all probability be able to show you one or two choice specimens, either in china or in bronze, of his household gods. And so strongly is the love of Nature impressed within him that he cannot pass a beautiful scene--a hillside of blossom, or a sunset--without stopping his ricksha to allow you also the privilege of enjoying it. Often when taking a drive in the country he will suddenly stop in front of some delightful scene, put down your ricksha, and, taking from his kimono sleeve a little roll of rice, wrapped in a dainty bamboo leaf, will sit down and begin to eat it with his chopsticks, continuing to gaze at the scene, every now and then looking up at you for sympathy. If you are an artist, and will look at the scene intelligently and appreciatively, this little ricksha man will be your slave for life and will do anything for you.

Men are esteemed in Japan in proportion to their artistic capabilities, and not for their banking accounts. It is in this quality of imagination that we Britishers are deficient. Our lack of imagination will be the cause of the decline of our Empire, if it does decline.

Then, the Japanese are a polite people. If you give a present to some little child, a mite strapped to the back of a sister that is scarcely bigger than itself, you are almost sure to find that little child waiting for you on your return to your hotel with some small trifle to offer you; and this little one will bow to you from its rather awkward position with all the grace imaginable. Two coolies sweeping the roads, when meeting for the first time in the day, will lay down their brooms and salute each other before passing on their way to work.

I have had many experiences, when sketching the streets of Japan, of the people's politeness. A policeman becoming interested in my work would help to keep clear a space in the road, and never dream of overlooking my work or of embarrassing me in any way. In one street of a village he actually had the traffic turned down another way, so as not to interfere with my sketching. Fancy a policeman in England diverting the traffic simply because an artist wanted to sketch a meat shop!

One of the most remarkable illustrations of the native politeness that I have ever witnessed was in Tokio. A man pulling along a cart loaded high up with boughs of trees chanced to catch the roof of a coolie's house in one of his pieces of timber, tearing away a large portion of it (for a roof is a very slim affair in Japan). The owner of the house rushed out thoroughly upset, and began to expostulate, and to explain how very distressing it was to have one's roof torn off in this manner. No doubt if he had been a Britisher he would have used quaint language; but there are no "swear words" in the Japanese language--they are too polite a people. The abused one stood calmly, with arms folded, listening to the harangue, and saying nothing. Only, when the enraged man had finished, he pointed to the towel which in his haste the coolie had forgotten to take off his head. At once the coolie realised the enormity of his offence. Both hands flew to the towel, and tore it off in confusion, the coolie bowing to the ground and offering humble apologies for having presumed to appear without uncovering his head. For in Japan one must always uncover, whether to a sweep or to a Mikado. The two parted the best of friends. One had been impolite enough to forget to uncover; the other had torn away a roof. The rudeness of the one balanced the injury of the other. Thus are offences weighed in Japan.

THE END